Direct Work with Children

Child Care Policy and Practice
Series Editor: Tony Hall
           Director and Secretary
           British Agencies for Adoption and Fostering

Direct Work with Children

A Guide for Social Work Practitioners

Edited by
JANE ALDGATE
and JOHN SIMMONDS

B.T. Batsford Ltd. *London*
in association with
British Agencies for Adoption and Fostering

For Hannah Aldgate and Rachel
and Adam Simmonds

© Jane Aldgate and John Simmonds 1988

First published 1988
Reprinted 1990

Typeset by Progress Fine Art, London EC1
Printed and bound in Great Britain by
Biddles Ltd, Guildford and King's Lynn

Published by B.T. Batsford Ltd
4 Fitzhardinge Street, London W1H 0AH

British Library Cataloguing in Publication Data

Aldgate, Jane
    Direct work with children : a guide for social work practitioners
    ——(Child care policy and practice).
    1. Children——Care and hygiene
    I. Title   II. Simmonds, John   III. Series
    362.7'95   RJ101

    ISBN 0–7134–5594–2

Contents

Foreword Helen Martyn

This book could not have been written without the impetus of Nessie Bailey and the pioneering work that she has done in working directly with children. For Nessie Bailey it was not good enough that plans and decisions were made (or sadly often *not* made) for children without any direct work being done with them. For her, moreover, such work was not a casual checking out of a foregone conclusion with a child, but rather a humble and sensitive entry into the child's world. Nessie's gift still lies in the way she is able to open herself up to the painful experiences and confusion of a child.

I knew about Nessie Bailey's work when I went to the BAAF Swanwick conference in 1983 where she was showing some of the work she had done with children. To call this an exhibition, which is technically correct, is to seriously misrepresent it. To call it an experience is more accurate, for it was an entrance into the world of damaged, abandoned or despairing young people. Perhaps it was because this work was displayed in a chapel that everyone spoke in soft voices, but I think it was also a product of the humility and distress evoked by such material. Painful as this work was, it was not depressing, for feelings of hope and the impulse towards growth were most certainly present too. Increasingly, Nessie has seen the main focus of her work as the teaching and training of others; and so, when planning the Goldsmiths' Course, we turned unequivocally to her for the first Direct Work with Children sequence. It was her teaching on this course which inspired much of the practice described in this book.

It is entirely appropriate that children are now coming to be seen as clients in their own right and that social workers are developing the skills to work with them. This book is intended as a contribution to this process and a tribute to the person who initiated it for a generation of social workers.

Acknowledgements

We are very grateful to all the students from the first three years of the Diploma in Advanced Social Work (Children and Families) at University of London Goldsmiths' College for providing the inspiration for this book. Our warm thanks go to all the contributors who worked so diligently. Helen Martyn as course convenor was instrumental in launching the course itself and provided the impetus for many of the ideas at the planning stages of this book. Without her, none of this could have happened. We also wish to thank Kathy Sylva for her advice and our colleagues who gave the time for us to do the work. We are also grateful to Sarah Curtis, Editor, *Adoption and Fostering* for permission to quote material. We could not have produced this book without the support and loyalty of our spouses or the tolerance of our children, who put up with our repeated absences with remarkable patience and acceptance. We owe them a great deal. Additionally, our thanks must go to Gail Simmonds for her meticulous help with the text and insight throughout. Finally, the book would not have reached the publisher without the perseverance of Suzanne Jones and her trusty Apple Macintosh from the Department of Social and Administrative Studies at Oxford University. Her production of the various drafts was an inspiration in itself.

The Contributors

Jane Aldgate
Jane Aldgate is a Lecturer in Applied Social Studies and Fellow of St Hilda's College, University of Oxford. She is actively involved in social work research and has completed several studies on children in care. She is also the author of many articles on child care research, policy and practice.

John Simmonds
John Simmonds is a Tutor and Senior Lecturer in Social Work at Goldsmiths' College, University of London. His principal interest is in the application of psychodynamic concepts to social work. In relation to these, he has been involved in work with staff groups in a number of child care agencies on practice as well as supervisory and management issues.

Margaret Adcock
Margaret Adcock is a freelance consultant social worker. She is a member of two panels of Guardian ad Litems, an Assistant Teacher at the Institute of Family Therapy and a Tutor and Lecturer on the Diploma in Advanced Social Work (Children and Families) at Goldsmiths' College. She has made a major contribution to the development, theory and practice of current child care policy and is the author of many notable publications.

Eva Banks
Eva Banks is a senior social worker in a children's team in the Social Services Department of the London Borough of Wandsworth. She specializes in work with children in long-term care and the supervision of workers doing direct work.

Nadine Brummer
Nadine Brummer is a Senior Lecturer in Social Work at Goldsmiths' College, University of London. Coming from an immigrant family herself, she has been consistently interested in issues of identity, race and culture. She has long-standing practice experience of social work with handicapped adolescents, adults and their families.

Peter Daniel
Peter Daniel is Coordinator of the Assessment and Resource Day Centre for Families and Children with the Social Services Department of the London Borough of Lewisham. This is a new project which seeks to provide children and families with intensive support to prevent disruption of placements.

Dominic Dubois
Dominic Dubois is a social worker with The Catholic Children's Society. He is principally interested in adoption and fostering, the counselling of adopted adults and direct work with children. He is a Guardian ad Litem.

Janet Galley
Janet Galley is a social worker in the family placement team in Bedfordshire Social Services Department. She specializes in work with children and families, planning for children in care and fostering and adoption.

Miles Hapgood
Miles Hapgood is a district manager in Devon Social Services Department. He has a longstanding specialist interest in work with children and families.

Eve Hopkirk
Eve Hopkirk is a family placement social worker in Surrey Social Services Department. Her main interests include adoption and direct work with children.

Roger Lake
Roger Lake is a team manager with the Social Services Department of the London Borough of Lewisham. His special interests are direct work with children, the maintaining of parental contact with children in care and preventative work and rehabilitation.

Gail Martin
Gail Martin is a senior social worker with the Social Services Department of the London Borough of Lewisham. She is particularly interested in direct work with children and has been involved in short projects including the production of a local guide-book for children in care.

Helen Martyn
Helen Martyn is a Senior Lecturer in Social Work at Goldsmiths' College. She has been central to the planning and development of the Diploma in Advanced Social Work (Children and Families). She is active in social work practice and is engaged in research on post-qualifying courses in social work.

Sarah Mumford
Like Eva Banks, Sarah Mumford is a social worker in a children's team in the Social Services Department of the London Borough of Wandsworth. She has a particular interest in direct work and planning for children in care.

Venetia Pigott
Venetia Pigott is a group worker in a family support centre in West Kent, where she specializes in running therapeutic groups, including one for severely disturbed children.

Andrew Small
Andrew Small is a team leader with the Reading division of Berkshire Social Services Department. He runs a children and families' group and specializes in child care planning and direct work with children.

Introduction *Jane Aldgate and John Simmonds*

This book had its origin in a conversation over lunch at Goldsmiths' College in 1985, following the examination of students for the second year of the Advanced Diploma in Social Work with Children and Families. Both the tutors, Helen Martyn, John Simmonds, Margaret Adcock and Nadine Brummer, and the external examiner, Jane Aldgate, had been very impressed with the submissions of the sixteen students from each year. Several were outstanding as examples of direct work with children and would provide useful guidance for others about to begin this kind of work. From this beginning, the book began to take shape. Appropriately, it is a combined effort from teachers and students, with the aim of providing a theoretical framework informed by examples from practice.

John Simmonds begins the book with an evaluation of the main issues surrounding social work with children. In Chapter 2, Margaret Adcock provides a framework for assessment of children, using Roger Lake's meticulous information-gathering and Andrew Small's awareness of the need for preparation before embarking on direct work. Jane Aldgate's Chapter 3 sets the scene for the themes of loss and separation which permeate the book. These are taken up in Chapter 4, where Jane Aldgate and John Simmonds use the work of Peter Daniel, Gail Martin and Venetia Pigott to demonstrate the diversity of forms of direct work with children who have been emotionally damaged, and their potential for partial or complete recovery. Chapter 4 also emphasizes the importance in any direct work of appropriately involving the adults in children's lives. Even though the work may be varied, one factor is common to all the children, the need to involve their families in intervention. This issue is endorsed in Chapter 5 by Jane Aldgate who, with help from Janet Galley, looks at the issues involved in finding permanent families for older children. In Chapter 6 Nadine Brummer considers the critical concept of transcultural social work and the impact on children's identity. In Chapter 7 Miles Hapgood takes social work into the computer age by showing how life story work can be made very relevant for adolescents. No social work can be undertaken properly without supervision and it is appropriate that a Goldsmiths' supervisor, Eva Banks, and her colleague Sarah Mumford should write of their experiences in Chapter 8. Recognizing further the complexity of direct work, Eve Hopkirk in Chapter 9 provides guidance for social workers on how they may obtain further training before embarking on direct work. Appropriately perhaps, the volume is brought to a close by Margaret Adcock's Chapter 10, which recognizes the importance of ending relationships properly, illustrated by work from Andrew Small and Dominic Dubois.

The themes of the book are, we hope, explicit. They include the value of flexible permanency planning, the need for preparation, setting of boundaries and a sound knowledge base before work begins, and the valuing of the relationship between child and worker as an enabling part of the work and a recognition of its emotional content.

Many of the ideas which inspired the students came from Nessie Bailey's teaching on direct work methods on the Goldsmiths' Diploma course. Her charisma and creativity permeates the students' account of their work. We hope, above all, that the central concern shown throughout this book is respect for the children themselves, whose experiences of sadness, loss and rejection led to the need for social work intervention in the first place. They too have a lot to teach us.

1 Social Work with Children: Developing a Framework for Responsible Practice *John Simmonds*

The diploma course at Goldsmiths' College, for qualified social workers specialising in work with children and families, was first presented in 1984. A one-year, part-time course, it had been developed jointly by staff from BAAF (British Agencies for Adoption and Fostering) and social work lecturers from Goldsmiths' and from Chelsea College. Much of the impetus for the course can be traced back to Rowe and Lambert's seminal book *Children Who Wait* (1973), to Goldstein, Freud and Solnit's *Beyond the Best Interest of the Child* (1973), to the impact of enquiries into the death of children such as Maria Colwell (1972) in local authority care, and to rapid changes in the law relating to children. The development of policy and practice in both America and Britain to deal with these issues has been important as well, and can be most clearly identified in the idea of *permanency planning* (Maluccio 1986, Adcock 1980).

In principle, the concept of permanency planning for children should sharpen the thoughts and practice of those involved in child care work. However, the notion that social workers become pro-active in their interventions in child care cases can contrast significantly with the long established and well embedded social work values of acceptance and client self-determination. This fundamental change in approach to clients has seemed difficult to many, and the additional demand for rapid assessment, decision making and legal remedy for children in care has produced much further controversy. Even if the policy of permanency is founded on critical psychological concepts like attachment and bonding, and clearly stated legal concepts like 'first consideration to the need to safeguard and promote the welfare of the child throughout his childhood' (section 18, Child Care Act 1980), the balance between the needs of children and the rights of birth parents is

1

painfully difficult to maintain in practice. However, while the dilemmas surrounding this balance continue to be actively debated, local authorities with established permanency policies, and individual social workers influenced by the same ideas, are actively working to re-establish children with their natural parents, or to prepare them for, or establish them in, foster or adoptive homes. This has raised an important and in some respects new set of issues regarding the need to prepare children for rehabilitation or placement by working with them directly, in their own right.

The need to work directly with children in care is long established but, at the current time, the concept of doing so is in a state of rapid development and change. Most fieldworkers, whenever they might have practised, will have experienced the discomfort of visits to children in residential homes. Ushered, embarrassed, into a special room set aside for such purposes, with all the weight of legal responsibility for the child, the social worker attempts to exercise some of the personal qualities which seem to set adults at ease, but finds the role of local authority aunt or uncle quickly brings about a rapid deterioration in the social atmosphere, resulting in something more akin to an interrogation with monosyllabic answers. This situation is eased somewhat by a visit to the local tea room for cakes or, in a more contemporary setting, by going to McDonalds. However, statutory responsibility and adult social skills are no way to children's hearts, and even if this caricature does little justice to some of the excellent individual work done over the years, the scenario will be recognised by many. The problems of knowing what to do with children – and for what reason – are legion. These problems have been accentuated by the need to ascertain the wishes of children before any decisions are made and by the need to make clear and full assessment of their future best interests. Passive visiting of children in residential or foster homes is no longer acceptable within a culture of pro-active child care work (see Marsh and Fisher 1986, Vernon and Fruin 1985).

It is becoming increasingly necessary, therefore, to begin to develop a framework for the practice of direct work with children. While there is considerable interest in such work, and a reasonable amount of material available on the subject, there is also confusion and uncertainty about objectives, focus and techniques. The problem with developing such a framework, and being clear about its boundaries, is that while it relates to the accepted role of the social worker in child protection and child placement, working directly with children crosses into the field of child psychiatry, child psychotherapy and educational and clinical psychology. As such, it raises a complex set of issues, for, if the principles and objectives are broadly clear in terms of the social worker's role in effecting transitions and re-establishing or establishing new attachments for the child, the context within which this takes place is the extraordinarily painful experience of neglect, abuse and rejection suffered by many children in care, and their resultant behavioural, emotional, learning and social problems. Direct work therefore involves serious questions about what social workers might realistically and responsibly undertake with children. It has to be admitted that the answers to these questions are as yet unclear. Indeed the problem is not confined to this particular area of work, for the range of objectives that social workers have with any of their client groups can be very wide – from the intensely therapeutic to the immensely practical.

So, while there are some individual workers and some social work agencies with much experience and interest in direct work with children, and while there are a number of published books and articles which discuss techniques for doing so, there is a need at the present time for an evaluation of the current position in order to give some direction to future developments.

The question of responsibility in child care practice is extensively explored in the third volume of Goldstein et al's trilogy. Discussing the responsibility of the professionals involved, they say,

> We believe that they [professionals] would agree that they ought not to exceed their authority and ought not to go beyond or counter to their special knowledge or training. But we do not take for granted that they always recognize when they go or are asked to go beyond their limits. Sometimes they do not recognize that they are doing what they 'know' they ought not to do. This may be because the law gives them vague and ambiguous assignments; because they have a strong desire to help people in trouble; because they feel a need to justify their work; because they desire to avoid the embarrassment of acknowledging that they do not know; because they do not pause to consider whether they are being asked to exceed their professional qualifications; or because of a combination of these and other less obvious or, perhaps, less understandable reasons. (Goldstein, et al, 1986, p 7)

The problem is therefore similar to that which arises in many other areas of practice in social work – what limits should be set for social workers working directly with children? When theories and techniques are now available at the turn of a page, how can social workers ensure that the work they do with children is well founded, within the limitations of their competence and training, and supported by their agency? This chapter is only a beginning in trying to answer some of these questions. It is also a framework against which some of the work described in later chapters might be understood. As such, the chapter has three sections:

1 What is currently known about social workers and their contact with children.
2 The role of the social worker in direct work with children.
3 A discussion of some of the current ideas and practice in direct work with children.

The Current Position

The current debate about policy and practice in child care is of major importance: we need to resolve the issue of children drifting in care, and raise the standard of service offered to one of the most vulnerable groups in society. While the concept of permanency has become over-identified with adoption, at the expense of other forms of substitute care, and, most particularly, at the expense of preventative policies and services to natural families, the appropriate use of foster and adoptive placements is still a significant part of any such policy. However, placing children in long-term foster or adoptive homes is clearly neither simple nor straightforward. Whether it is the debate about the form that fostering takes, as in the 'exclusive fostering vs. inclusive fostering argument' (Holman 1975; also Fox 1982), or about the recruitment, status or support of foster parents, or the relationship between fostering and adoption, there is much evidence to suggest that while placing children in families rather than in residential care is the dominant policy in most child care agencies, it is a high-risk activity. The figure of 50% disruption in foster home placements is much quoted in literature based on research carried out in the 1950s and 1960s (Trasler 1960; Parker 1966; George 1970; Napier 1972). More recent figures are variable. In a study of South Devon (Tibbenham 1982) a figure of 40–50% is quoted, while for the London Borough of Haringey (Haringey 1982) a figure of 24% is given. Essex Social Services Department give a figure of 14% (Essex 1982). In one of the most recent studies (Rowe et al 1984) a success rate of 52% is quoted for children under two, 32% for children aged two to four and 16% for children over five. Noting the very much younger age of children in their study in comparison to the studies of the sixties, they still found that the overall figure for successful placements was very similar.

For many children the instability of placements is a major feature of their lives. Rowe et al (1984) found, for example, that, for 83% of the children in their sample, the current placement was not their first, although for 70% it was their only admission into care. In Packman's (1986) study, 80% of children had moved more than twice and 25% four or more times in just a few months. Similar figures are available from Fisher et al (1986) and Millham et al (1985). Another significant factor is the increased likelihood of disruption in the first year (Soothill 1981, West 1982). Given the problem of defining foster breakdown and of drawing valid comparisons between research studies, Rowe et al conclude that

> the verdict on long-term fostering is 'not proven'. In spite of many positive aspects, too many of the study placements had drifted from being short-term or indefinite into an undeclared permanency . . . It was our very strong impression that, although many of the placements we studied were working well, they were doing so in spite of the system rather than because of it. (Rowe et al, 1984, p 224)

Whatever the reason for the high level of disruption in foster placements, practice wisdom would suggest that preparation of the child for placement is a crucial factor. The DHSS warned in 1976 about the dangers of fostering practice becoming arrangement-dominated rather than child-orientated, and of the need for social workers to 'train themselves in the discipline of observing and understanding the meaning of what they see and hear. To this end they must spend time with the child' (DHSS 1976, p 73). Social workers need to recognise that for children to return to their families of origin or make attachments to a new family, is not just a matter of administrative arrangement. It is a complex process, involving emotional as well as practical issues; the past, present and future may need considerable attention, and this may require direct intervention. In essence, children have to be sufficiently resolved about the past, or in the process of resolving the past, to feel safe enough and motivated enough to reinvest in their birth families or make an investment in new families.

It is also clear that preparation is not the only point at which social workers should have direct contact with children. Children have an on-going need for information about themselves and their families of origin; they must be given an opportunity to discuss any plans that they, their birth parents or new parents or the social services department might have for their future. It has also been made manifestly clear in recent public inquiries that this activity is not optional; when parental rights are held by social services departments, social workers are obliged to discharge their responsibilities with full recognition of their status as legal parents. In a telling passage from the Beckford Inquiry, the committee says,

> Throughout the three years of social work with the Beckfords, Ms. Wahlstrom totally misconceived her role as the field worker enforcing Care Orders in respect of two very young children at risk. Her gaze was focussed on Beverley Lorrington and Morris Beckford; she averted her eyes to the children to be aware of them only as and when they were with their parents, hardly ever to observe their development, and never to communicate with Jasmine on her own. The two children were treated as mere appendages to their parents who were treated as the clients, although Ms. Wahlstrom did tell the Magistrates in 1981 that her 'primary role is the welfare of the children.' (In the meticulous record of nearly 100 pages of detailed notes kept by Ms. Wahlstrom and others in the Social Worker's Report there is not a single entry devoted exclusively to Jasmine and Louise). (Blom-Cooper 1985, p 293)

The objective is clear: social workers are in many instances obliged by law, and even where they are not, by the principles of good practice, to work directly with children.

Yet evidence from other research suggests that the tragic example of Jasmine Beckford is certainly not an isolated one (Vernon and Fruin 1985, Millham et al 1985, Rowe et al 1984). In a Norfolk study, 50% of children fostered were found to be receiving only the minimum number or less of statutory visits. Triseliotis (1980), in his study of foster children, found a significant absence of frequent, continued and planned contact between social worker and child. While Rowe et al (1984) found that nearly two-thirds of social workers reported seeing the children for whom they were responsible in the previous year, this is hardly an inspiring record. However, on further investigation it became apparent that a far smaller number of these children reported seeing their social worker alone than the social workers themselves had reported, something that was significantly supported by a number of the foster parents in the sample. Rowe et al conclude,

> The only explanation seemed to be that the 'seeing alone' was often very brief and passed unnoticed by child and foster parent. It could still, of course, provide an opportunity for the child to speak confidentially to the social worker if he or she wished to do so, but it was evidently not something that the child could look forward to or count on.' (Rowe et al 1984, p 159).

It is important to note in this context that 80% of foster parents in this study welcomed or did not object to social workers seeing their foster children alone.

Whatever the explanation for this poor record of contact between social workers and children, the evidence from research, together with the results of public inquiries, demand that improvements be made to the training and practice of social workers where children are concerned.

The Role of the Social Worker in Direct Work with Children

There is little evidence to help determine to what degree preparation is critical in establishing and maintaining a placement that does not disrupt, and how far it is important in terms of improving the quality of life for the child in its own right. However, practice wisdom and critical concepts like attachment, separation and loss suggest that preparation of the child is vital (Fratter et al 1982, Fitzgerald et al 1982a). However, it is also important to remember that evidence from researchers such as Rowe et al (1984) and Aldgate and Hawley (1986) indicates that in the great majority of cases, children are placed with little systematic assessment of their needs and with little information passed on to foster parents, even about their daily routines.

Horne (1983) outlines the three principal tasks involved in preparing a child for adoption, which could apply to any placement:

1 Learning about his view of himself and his experiences so that this knowledge can be shared with the prospective adopters.
2 Becoming familiar with him and his world and meeting and talking with the people who are important to him.
3 Building a relationship with the child which will enable him to work on the other parts of the task and move to a new family.

The essence of the social worker's role, in Horne's terms, is 'building a bridge for the child'. This definition fits easily with other conceptions of the social worker's role in enabling children to make transitions from one situation to another, and accords with developments in ecological theories of social work intervention. Permanency planning, in America in particular, has taken issue with approaches to child welfare and placement which have the psychopathology of parents and children as a basis for assessment, decision-making and placement. It is for this reason that the ecological approach has appeared so attractive, with its strong emphasis on the interaction of human beings with the environment, and on behaviour as functionally adaptive to the environment, as well as its focus on strength and health rather than illness and dysfunction. Maluccio et al say,

> Rather than relying primarily on traditional psychotherapeutic techniques such as insight orientated procedures, workers should become experts in methods of environmental modification, use of existing resources and natural helping networks, creation of new resources that may be needed by their clients and mobilization of family members' own resources. (Maluccio et al 1986 p 85)

This trend is very much in line with developments in family therapy, and, in Britain, with the development of community social work. The notion of reinforcing a family's own strengths and coping skills to deal with the many complex tasks facing them (Gambrill, 1983) has a hopeful and positive ring that is missing in many other theories of intervention.

The positive emphasis in this approach, and the idea of social workers acting as a bridge in the placement of children, also help emphasize the importance of the network of people in a child's life, and the fact that direct work cannot be successfully done in a vacuum. It is something that needs to be planned and coordinated in relation to the overall plan for the child, and in cooperation with the other significant adults in the child's life. However, while in principle the concept of 'networking' might help focus the social worker's role in child care work, and in some senses seem relatively uncontroversial, it does touch on a very controversial area – that of parental access and contact.

Studies such as Millham et al (1985), Aldgate (1980), and Fanshel and Shinn (1978) suggest that the degree of contact between a child in care and his or her family of origin is one of the best guides to the likelihood of successful rehabilitation. Millham also suggests that in those instances where a child does not return home to his natural parents, his psychological, social and educational adjustment is far better when regular parental contact is maintained. However, where it does occur, he says it is largely left to chance by social workers, who often find it difficult to keep up with what can often be a rapidly changing family membership – a factor identified in other research (see Fisher et al 1986).

While Millham et al's research is recent, it is only one more addition to the long debate between those who argue that parental contact is an important and beneficial part of a fostering arrangement (Family Rights Group 1982, British Association of Social Workers 1982) and those who argue that such contact makes a significant contribution to disruption because a foster family needs the security that comes through having total control over the children it has in its care (BAAF 1984, Tizard

1977, Goldstein et al 1973). Summaries of these debates are to be found in Fox (1982). However, while the significance of parental contact continues to be a controversial issue, the need for children to know about their past and be able to incorporate this within the development of their identity is less controversial, although not without difficulties (Triseliotis 1973).

In his study of 40 children who had grown up in foster care, Triseliotis (1980) found that 35% of both children and parents had what he terms mutually satisfying relationships. In these families, the foster parents' openness about the child's status, and their willingness both to share information and encourage parental contact, was, while sometimes painful, appreciated by and important to the child. This contrasted markedly with those for whom the relationship between foster parent and child had become seriously problematic. In this group, children remarked on the impatience, inaccessibility, lack of sensitivity and unpredictability of their foster parents. Four out of this group of five children did not know about their status until they were over seven. Furthermore, Triseliotis found that information about the child's origins was used in a critical and rejecting way to explain difficulties with the child's behaviour.

The lack of information passed to foster parents and to foster children is striking in a number of studies (Rowe et al 1984, Fitzgerald 1979, Thorpe 1974). Rowe and her colleagues comment,

> The paucity of information held by most (long term) foster parents was most striking. 20% did not know where the child was born, nearly a third were ignorant of the mother's first name, and overall 56% had less than five items of information from a basic list (of 10). (Rowe et al 1984, p 130)

When the children in the study were asked to say something about their natural parents, 28% could give no information at all about their mothers, another 38% could only produce one or two pieces of information, while only 33% could offer three or more. A similar lack of knowledge prevailed about the reasons why they were in care. The children did not lack curiosity about their original families and what they looked like, but Rowe reports that they did find it difficult to ask questions about them. This picture is disturbing, given the importance of knowledge about one's origins for every individual, and particularly for children separated from their birth families.

An increasing awareness of some of these issues has undoubtably had an important impact on the development in practice of life story work (Ryan and Walker 1985, Thom and Macliver 1986, Mitchell 1981). It is probably the most well known of the techniques available to direct work with children and also the most uncontroversial. If, as argued above, social workers have a primary responsibility for children in their care, and a duty to ensure both the development and maintenance of a coherent and meaningful sense of personal identity, history and culture, then life story work becomes essential. However, while the need for life story work is clear, many of the issues surrounding it are not. What to tell, when to tell and how to tell have to be considered alongside what the child wants to know, what the child can bear to hear and what makes sense to the child, given his or her chronological age and maturity. Whatever judgements a social worker might make about these, the exercise is still more than simply educational and the information itself more than just a collection of objective facts. As Zeitlin says, 'It is unfortunately all too easy to press destructive and unwanted information onto a vulnerable child who is just developing a personal identity and a good image' (Zeitlin, 1983, p 46). Life story work needs to be approached with the same sensitivity and skill as any other form of social work intervention dealing with vulnerable people.

However, the development of life story work focuses not just on the child's need to know about his or her past as part of the development of identity, but also on the need to know in order to come to terms with the past and then to be able to make a transition into a new family. It is for this reason that the concepts of loss and separation, and the theory of bereavement counselling, have been important (Jewett 1984). As such, direct work can have an explicit therapeutic objective, with social workers being concerned not just with acting as a bridge but also with directly intervening in some of the underlying behavioural, emotional and learning difficulties of the child involved (see Curtis 1982, Fitzgerald et al 1982a, Fratter et al 1982).

The evolution of this work also brings with it a development in the role of the social worker. No longer is he or she straddling the legal, administrative and emotional boundary of the complex network involved in placing a child, either back home or in a new family; the social worker has become rather a therapeutic agent in one part of it, by working directly with the child. While this latter issue is to be further discussed in this chapter, it is important to note that at the present time there is little obvious agreement about the appropriateness of who actually takes responsibility for what. Indeed, Rowe's research (Rowe et al 1984) shows that there is some disagreement between the views of social workers and foster parents with regard to who has the primary responsibility for sharing family history with the child. While 25% of social workers thought that they were primarily responsible, only 2% of foster parents agreed with this, and only 25% of foster parents saw social workers as having any role at all. While it is important not to use what people feel as the only indicator of what might actually be good practice, it is important for social workers, when undertaking any work that involves a network of people, to consider the impact of that work on the network as a whole. As one part of this, it is clearly necessary to consider who is the best person to undertake such work and this may well not be the social worker. However, while the issue of the role of the social worker is still one that requires further debate, particularly where it concerns the area of life story work, there are other developments which add to the complexity of the current position.

Knowing the facts about one's past is a necessary part of the development of a sense of personal history, identity and culture. However, giving a child an opportunity to get to know these facts is different from giving a history lesson at school. As has already been highlighted, it also clearly has the aim of being a kind of therapy, in that it gives the child an opportunity through expressing feelings associated with the past to lay claim to important parts of personal, family and cultural history and to set some of what remains to rest.

The need for therapeutic work is made very clear in some of the research into the characteristics of children in care. Triseliotis (1980) found that foster parents had to cope with a significant amount of difficult behaviour, or with particularly difficult conditions at the time of placement, including temper tantrums, enuresis, epileptic fits, mental retardation, and passivity. Thorpe (1974) found that 37% of the children in her study were rated as seriously disturbed on Rutter's Behaviour Questionnaire. Rowe et al's 1984 study of 145 children in long-term foster care found that out of a list of problems including temper tantrums, lack of concentration, attention-seeking, stealing, lying, destructiveness, and sleeping difficulties, 60% of children aged one or below at the time of placement had no reported difficulties, while 54% of children aged one to four and 43% of children aged five or above had three or more problems at the time of placement. Many of the problems reported by these foster parents showed a persistence for many years into the placement (see also Keane 1983). Rowe and her colleagues also attempted to give a measure of adjustment for the children and young people in her study. They say, '21 out of 72 of the younger children (29%) showed some disorder . . . 15 out of 50 older

11

adolescents (30%) gave "cause for concern" . . . In all, therefore, we have 36 children (30%) who can be appropriately designated as giving cause for concern' (Rowe et al p 82). In spite of the difficulty of making direct comparisons between different studies, Rowe et al found that their group appeared to be less disturbed than those in other studies, but even as a minimum figure it is significantly higher than the quoted 7% figure for children in general in the Isle of Wight study (Rutter, Tizard and Whitmore 1970). Given the extent of the children's problems in their study, it is surprising to find that only 14 of the 145 (10%) had been seen by psychiatric or psychological clinics, with very few of them receiving treatment beyond an initial evaluation.

While the help offered to foster children and foster parents in this regard is lamentably poor, and the problems to be overcome quite extensive, a number of projects, particularly those offering a period of residential care prior to foster or adoptive placement, have tried to intervene directly to help children through some of these difficulties. For example, Dr Barnardo's Cambridge Cottage Pre-Fostering and Adoption Unit (Fratter et al 1982) describe their objectives as helping children to recover from the trauma of the breakdown of their family of origin. This can involve unravelling the past through the use of life story books, charting the moves that might have been made and the events that might have occurred throughout that child's life. Children also discuss with staff and each other their present circumstances, the reason for admission to the Unit, and their expectations, and fantasies, of what family placement means. Work is also undertaken to identify the children's needs and modify their behaviour. In a similar context, Fitzgerald et al say of the children referred to St Luke's,

> Most of them had suffered rejection by their families and came to us bearing the scars of their emotional wounds. Some of them had . . . lacked stimulation and opportunities for normal maturation and healthy relationships. We learned by experience that most of our children were too damaged to grow out of their difficulties without specific help. Treatment of their emotional problems was essential to future progress. (Fitzgerald et al 1982a, p 37)

The potential role of the social worker in child care work is therefore complex. While undoubtedly part of a network of services in an administrative, legal and professional framework, as well as part of the wider network of the client community, the exact part to be played by the social worker is still open to many interpretations. However, it is clear that the problems of many children coming into care are such that, whether direct responsibility is assumed for it or not, work has to be undertaken to identify and intervene in those problems. While life story work as a method has given considerable impetus to this, it is clear that the focus and objectives of such work are by no means simple to identify. This issue is explored in more detail in the third section.

Current Ideas and Practice in Direct Work with Children

The treatment approaches underpinning much of the work now undertaken are not very specific, but there are three main trends: the ecological, as described above; client centred/non-directive play therapy; and gestalt. A fourth, the psychoanalytic approach, is important, but as yet largely without influence, except in a historical sense. Other approaches are most certainly of significance – most notably behaviour therapy and family therapy – but these largely fall outside the current direct work paradigm.

Probably one of the few books to have made a significant impact on people working with children is Axline's classic text, *Dibs – In Search of Self* (1964). In her book, Axline allows the work she did with Dibs to speak for itself, largely without comment or interpretation from her. Her non-directive stance in relation to him, and her belief in his capacity to grow through his various difficulties, are powerfully attractive in their simplicity. However, they are also deceptive, because Axline's respect for and belief in Dibs, and her capacity not to allow her own wishes, feelings or anxiety to intrude into his discovery of himself, do not reflect the powerful feelings that children can stir up in therapists or social workers who want to protect them, rescue them or make things better. This capacity to contain one's own feelings is central to non-directive play therapy. Dorfman says,

> It is apparent that one of the more important personal qualities of a client centred play therapist must be the ability to tolerate silence without embarrassment. A therapist who feels rejected when the child fails to pour out his troubles will only add to the child's anxiety by his display of his own. (Dorfman 1965, p 247)

The maintenance of a non-directive stance, central to this approach, is therefore dependent on the capacity not to become embroiled in the emotional turmoil of a child's problems. This does, however, conflict with the powerful wish of most adults who have any feeling for children to rescue, protect or control them. This theme will be returned to later.

While there is little doubt about the influence of non-directive play

13

therapy on the thinking of social workers interested in working with children, it is probably the approach of the gestalt therapists, and the charismatic work and teaching of Nessie Bailey, disseminated through the BAAF teaching pack *In Touch with Children*, backed up by Oaklander (1978), Fahlberg (1981a, 1981b, 1982, 1984) and Jewett (1984), that has had the most recent practical impact on social workers.

A similar respect for children, and a belief in their creative and self-healing powers, underpins this approach. However, where Axline is strictly non-interventive, gestalt therapists like Oaklander interpret their role as taking a much more active part in helping children to express their inner feelings:

> It is up to me to provide the means by which we will open doors and windows to their inner worlds. I need to provide methods for children to express their feelings, to get what they are keeping guarded inside out into the open, so that together we can deal with this material. (Oaklander 1978, p 193)

Her book is a rich source of techniques and materials, and closely follows the gestalt therapist's concern with fantasy, projection and the central importance of experience, not as a clue to some '. . . "unconscious" unknown or symptom, but as the important thing itself' (Perls et al 1951, p 237).

This emphasis on 'getting at and getting out' what children feel is a central feature of much of the current literature available on direct work with children. Fitzgerald says, 'We learned . . . that the painful experiences of the past could not be left to sink into the unconscious to fester and cause later problems . . . but must be brought out into the open and dealt with' (Fitzgerald 1982, p 42). Similarly, Oaklander asserts, 'We can look into the inner realms of the child's being through fantasy. We can bring out what is kept hidden or avoided and we can also find out what's going on in the child's life' (Oaklander 1978, p 11). Hence much of the literature is focussed around three themes:

1 Children need to be able to communicate what they feel about what they have experienced – even if this is painful (and Oaklander feels this is so even if they are resistant).

2 That many children because of past experiences have blocked off the feeling part of them and hence do not have the means to know what they feel or the tools to express these feelings. Development of the senses – of the 'contact function' – looking, talking, touching, listening, moving, smelling and tasting has therefore become an important part of work with children and a significant part of the development of the sense of self.

3 There is a concern to provide children with the means to express what they feel – that they can be happy/good/angry/sad and have these feelings about important people in their past, present or future (Ryan and Walker 1985, p 19).

In part, this method is an education in the emotions (Fahlberg 1981b), as well as a recognition that many children have never, or seldom, had the experience of a caring, sensitive adult being concerned and interested in what they, from their own perspective, know, have felt and experienced. There can be little doubt of the therapeutic value of all children having contact with an adult with such qualities, and not just children in public care. However positive some of the objectives are, and creative as some of the techniques appear, there are some serious issues which also need consideration.

In a review of Lennox's book, *Residential Group Therapy for Children*, Shinegold (1983) says,

> It seems to me somewhat immoral to take techniques (transactional analysis, encounter group therapy, etc) that have been developed for the treatment of 'consenting' adults and apply them to a 'captive' group of children and young people. I do not deny that many children in care need help in recovering from the disturbing and sometimes devastating experiences that they have had, but the inappropriate emphasis on therapy that is still the fashion in far too many institutions is not a satisfactory answer to a child who is confused, lonely and unhappy. (Shinegold 1983, p 66)

Later, commenting on a chapter of 'games' designed to release feelings and fantasies, Shinegold adds,

> Having witnessed the same techniques used with groups of adults and seen some of them emerge in varying stages of shock and distress, I feel anxious that some residential workers may find themselves in the centre of a situation that has gone beyond their control. But theirs is only a minor problem compared with that of the children who are left raw and exposed with no relief from their pain which has been brought to consciousness but left unresolved. (Shinegold 1983, p 67)

While the reservations expressed by Shinegold do not amount to a rejection of the approaches he is reviewing, they do help to stress the considerable caution that needs to be exercised. These reservations also highlight the need to try to be clear about the scope and the depth of any therapeutic interventions that social workers might undertake. Indeed Sawbridge (1983) and Oaklander (1978) both question the use of the word 'therapeutic' to describe the relationship between worker and child, as well as the appropriateness of making interpretations for the child.

Social work theory has been persistently troubled by the question of how far social workers might appropriately go in trying to bring about change. This issue became critical in the 1950s, when social workers attempted to build up a practice model based on psychoanalytic thought. While at that time recognition was given to the importance of the unconscious in determining behaviour, intervening directly in the sphere of the unconscious, and making direct use of such phenomena as transference, were not acceptable. The important thing for the validity of social work was that recognition was given to a more comprehensive brief than that of the analytic couch and the consulting room. Yet the awareness of deeper psychological issues could not be easily set aside. The distinction between the social worker's concern with reality, with what is conscious and the social world, as opposed to the inner world, phantasy and the unconscious – the province of the psychoanalyst – did attempt to set a conceptual boundary for social work theory in the 1950s. However, such distinctions then required social workers to have a particularly firm grip on their own sense of reality, on their purpose, boundary, role and personal limitations. A similar problem exists now in direct work with children. It is equally important to have a firm grip on the objective and focus of such work, yet some of the current theoretical approaches do not help in clarifying the distinctions between what social workers and therapists can responsibly aspire to do.

As described above, the implicit assumption in client-centred play therapy and the explicit description of the role of the gestalt therapist is that the worker is a 'guide', passive in the case of the former, active in the case of the latter. However, as a definition of a role for social workers, this is inadequate and unhelpful. Untrained and inexperienced as most social workers normally are in the theory and practice underpinning these approaches, the idea of the expression of feelings as an end in themselves, unrelated to any clear analysis of what they mean in the structure of the personality, may be unhelpful. Moreover, the theories themselves do not sufficiently emphasize the importance of the relationship between social worker and child, and the impact and consequences of its development. It is not just that the available literature fails to emphasize the powerful feelings that can be stirred up in workers as a result of dealing directly with children; there is also considerable emphasis placed on the need for workers to be in touch with the pleasures and pains of their own childhood – indeed this is a central feature of much of the *In Touch With Children* teaching pack (BAAF 1984). What is not fully recognised is the power of these eelings to influence and determine, perhaps inappropriately, the objectives and content of the sessions and any techniques that might be used. In particular it is the unconscious processes and their effect on the interaction between worker and client and the part that these play in the work that is, as yet, unrecognised.

The dilemma for social workers engaging in direct work with children is that the relationship between worker and child – the means by which any work is done – is also capable of evoking a range of feelings, some of which will be associated with other relationships, particularly relationships with parental figures. These feelings can, in turn, become re-enacted in the relationship between worker and child in such a way as to seriously distort that relationship. In some cases, this can threaten to confirm for both worker and child the hopelessness of ever attempting to make a trusting and significant relationship. While some of the negative effects of re-enactment are clearly to be avoided, current psychoanalytic thinking places considerable importance on the feelings induced in the worker, and their use to help understand some of the difficulties the child has experienced and the way that they have become incorporated in its personality structure.

In a particularly vivid example, Gianna Henry, a psychoanalytically trained psychotherapist, describes the therapy of Martin, a 14-year-old boy who had attempted suicide one year before his 10-year foster placement disrupted. Martin was described as dangerously aggressive towards children in his school, and by one teacher as 'the only person he has come across who has no feelings.' Gianna Henry describes the contemptuous, cold and hard way in which Martin treated her as therapist and the pressure he put her under to give up trying to make contact with him. She says, 'I think that the very forceful impact he had on people in this respect must have deprived him many times of positive experiences. He had developed a talent not only for hardening himself, but for hardening people around him.' Henry then comes to see Martin not just as somebody who has been deprived of vital early parental contact, with understandably powerful feelings about the mother who has abandoned him. Rather, through her experience of the way he treats her in therapy, Henry comes to understand Martin by realising that he had taken inside himself an image of the vain, self-centred and hard mother. In becoming identified with her, Martin is able to defend himself against the feeling of being a small, vulnerable and dependent baby. These defences have the effect of putting Henry as therapist in the position of a 'child trying to make contact with

17

somebody who had no time to listen' – a reversal of the explicit therapeutic objective of providing Martin, as a needy young person, with someone who does have the time to listen. Henry comments:

> The purpose of Martin's unreachable attitude was then . . . to split and project into somebody else both the feelings he could not tolerate and a part of himself, the needy child he had to disown, while he identified himself with the unavailable mother whom at this time he idealized. (Henry, 1977, pp 317–318)

The importance of this example is that it stresses that children's feelings about their past experiences cannot be understood in any simple sense. Martin undoubtedly had feelings about the mother that abandoned him – he had come to identify with and idealize her. His feelings of abandonment and rejection had become incorporated within the structure of his personality in a very complex way, so that he came to embody the characteristics of the abandoning mother. Thus, the people he came into contact with came to feel some of his experience of being a rejected child. In this sense, past experiences are not 'out there', with the feelings about them a kind of 'emotional baggage' to be 'got out', discarded or even 'worked through' before a successful placement can be made. Rather, they need to be understood as something *inside*, possibly incorporated as a part of the defensive structure of the personality, a part of identity and the sense of self, directing what is perceived and what is acted upon. The dilemma for anybody working with a young person like Martin, whether an experienced therapist like Gianna Henry, or the teacher who had found Martin so 'unfeeling', or the foster parents who had provided him with a home for ten years, is that the more one tries to offer him, the more opportunity this provides for him, unless the basic nature of his defensive system is understood, to reinforce his identification with the rejecting mother and distance himself from the abandoned and rejected child.

Martin's difficulties are replicated in much of the therapeutic work with children described in Boston and Szur (1983). There is considerable emphasis on the pressure that very well trained psychotherapists can be put under by the intensity of the feelings conveyed during therapy. The fusing of the child's wishes or defences with the therapist's unconscious motivation to repair damaged relationships from his or her own past, poses a considerable risk to the successful outcome of any therapeutic work. It is also clear in Boston and Szur that a similar concern ought to be felt about the risk of children's earlier problems being re-enacted not just in therapy but also in any new placement, when rejected or abandoned children bring about through their behaviour a re-enactment of the very situation they fear (see Chapter 2).

The central feature of much of the discussion about these problems in Boston and Szur is the capacity of therapists not only to tolerate the powerful feelings induced in them by children, without acting upon them, but also to think about and understand these feelings. This capacity to analyse unwanted and unbearable feelings, and put them into words, is critical in turning them into something that can be tolerated and finally incorporated into a child's identity. This closely follows modern psychoanalytic thought on the developmental importance of the mother as a 'container' for the baby's unbearable feelings (Bion 1962).

The above discussion does not provide any easy answers for social workers undertaking direct work. The almost desperate need for such work to be done, and the increasing availability of relatively easily assimilated techniques, such as life story work, have to be tempered by a realization of the difficulties for both worker and child in developing a close and significant relationship. The pressure on social workers to stay within the theoretical limits of their role is at odds with the reality of children and families in trouble, presenting complex issues that do not easily succumb to rational discussion or understanding. Life story work, for example, can at one level be conceived of quite simply in terms of dealing with the facts of a child's life, and, in the process, helping children in a limited and safe way to express, at their own pace, some of their feelings about their history. The temptation, however, when confronted with a troubled, confused, frightened or lonely child, is to want to protect and rescue that child; this can easily lead social workers to offer more than is helpful or realistic.

The importance of the psychoanalytic model is not now, any more than it was in the 1950s and 1960s, that it provides a comprehensive framework for social work practice with children. Many of the more recent developments, particularly life story work, provide a more appropriate model for practice. But, as in the past, it is not possible to ignore the significance of the worker–child relationship and the possibility that even the most determined worker may become embroiled in the unconscious dynamics of the situation being worked with. This is significant whether the approach is non-directive, as with Axline, or active, as with Oaklander. The problem now, as then, is to develop sufficient insight and comprehension of these processes without the advantage of having embarked on either personal therapy or analytically based training.

Summary

Assessing and advising social workers on the appropriateness of what is done, to whom and at what depth is still problematic. The central theme and motivating force behind child care work is a recognition of children's primary needs for an open, sensitive, warm and caring adult in an appropriately safe physical environment. For all children therefore the primary therapeutic experience – the experience that allows them to grow – is, in fact, *family life*, in whatever form that might take. The development of sensitive permanency policies is clearly aimed at providing this for those children who cannot be with their families of origin. The development of direct work with children is only one part of this wider trend. It gives recognition to the need not just for assessment, and the finding and preparation of the placement, but also to the need for work that might enable such children to come to terms with the past, and appreciate and cope with new parents and a new family life when it becomes available.

It is important, in making these summarising statements, not to lose sight of the evidence outlined in the first part of this chapter regarding the paucity and low standard of many services offered to children in care, in particular where direct work with children is involved. Clearly some of this can be explained in terms of the absence of a culture of direct work with children in social work practice, which is also reflected in its absence from basic training courses. In turn, this is reflected in the lack of support for such work within the management of social work departments from committees downwards – 'playing with kids is not a good use of scarce resources'. It is also echoed by the absence of the physical space, the materials, and the time to do such work. None of these factors can in any way be discounted in the obstacle course to establish direct work, but other factors exist too which are of equal relevance and also need discussion.

One problem arises from the very strong feelings that children, and particularly children in care, stir up in social workers at a personal level – feelings that are invariably connected to their own childhood experiences. A second problem is in finding a way of communicating with children. A third difficulty is that literature on the subject tends either to be dauntingly hard to assimilate into practice – particularly the child psychotherapy literature – or that it oversimplifies complex matters through the eloquence of the written word. A fourth problem is that of the 'real child': children can be very off-putting to talk to about some of the painful areas in their lives. What might start out as 'direct work' can feel very indirect as one gets into it. Yet despite all these obstacles there are many examples in the following chapters showing how students on the Goldsmiths' Diploma in Advanced Social Work Course managed to overcome some of the problems in establishing direct work in their agencies and in their own practice. There is a need for further development of a conceptual, practical and responsible framework for direct work with children which is also adequately researched. What follows is intended as a contribution towards this.

2 Assessing Children's Needs

Margaret Adcock

with Roger Lake and Andrew Small

A Framework for Assessment

Children on social workers' caseloads have often had traumatic experiences of abuse, loss, separation and discontinuity. The social worker's task is firstly to protect these children from further risk, and secondly, to try and create a favourable environment for their recovery and future growth. The most important objective for social workers is to offer children a permanent family who can provide them with secure attachments, opportunities for enjoyment, and increased self-esteem, as well as activities to facilitate growth, development and the mastery of new skills. The role of the social worker is to help parents, or those who are to care for the child, to understand the way in which earlier developmental needs have not been met, and to help them provide good enough parenting in the future. It may also involve helping children to identify any feelings they may have about past events, and aiding them in making sense of any confusion they might have about these.

Studies of children coming into care suggest that the key factors which seem to put them most at risk are:

- a number of changes of placement
- the instability of the home and the rejection of those caring for the child
- the child's perception of the impermanence of their present home

Children themselves, however, can precipitate family breakdown by their behaviour, and their misinterpretations of situations. There is a continuous process of interaction between children and the significant people in their social world. For example, the separation of children from adults to whom they have been very attached may, in consequence, cause them to behave in ways that other adults find intolerable. As a result, these adults become unwilling or unable to provide the continuity of care which the child longs for (see Martin in Chapter 1 and Richard in Chapter 4). Wolkind (1984) described a study he undertook of children in residential care, where a considerable continuity of disorder was found over a five-year period. He concluded that the children's original disorder influenced the care system in such a way as to actually create conditions which then *increased* the disorder.

To plan a permanent family life for a child, therefore, social workers must not only recognise the importance of providing continuity of care, but also the importance of assessing children's difficulties in the context of their history, their home circumstances, their school situation and the effect of past decisions made by professionals about them. As Herbert (1985) points out, the term 'problem child' is an over-simplification; it makes it sound as though the problem belongs to the child alone, whereas it may be the 'problem situation' which needs attention. A treatment plan should be based on assessment of the child, his or her environment and the interaction between the two. The case study of 'Clifford' in this chapter demonstrates how the worker paid constant attention to this interaction.

To make an assessment it is necessary to acquire factual information from files and records, to observe and talk with children, parents, professionals workers and others concerned with the children's welfare. Assessing children means getting to know them and creating an atmosphere of trust in which they feel free to communicate both verbally and non-verbally. To this end, play is likely to be one important mcdium of communication.

Preparation and Assessment

Workers need to prepare themselves for working with a child. There are two steps which must always be taken. The first is to clarify the presenting problem and ask why an assessment is required at this time. The presenting problem may be:

- concern that the child's current living situation is not 'good enough'. The child may be experiencing rejection, neglect and physical, sexual or emotional abuse. An assessment of both the child and his/her situation is necessary to ascertain whether parenting is 'good enough'.

- the child's behaviour, which is causing concern and which may lead to a request for removal from his/her family or placement and prevent return.
- the child may have had a traumatic experience, accompanied by loss or separation. An assessment is necessary as a basis for plans to provide the child with opportunities for recovery and 'good enough' care in the future.
- the child may be in an impermanent placement. An assessment is necessary in order to plan a placement which can be permanent.

The second step is to prepare oneself. Andrew Small writes:

It is a basic casework principle and is part of the way one sees a client as a unique individual. If the worker has not prepared, 'cleared the decks', then he/she is not going to be able to truly engage that client as there will be too much psychological clutter getting in the way. In my work with Michael, I did this by:

(a) giving myself enough time and space to do the work. This meant negotiating with management for the 'space' on my caseload as well as preparing the real space, the working playroom.

(b) booking the sessions, so that they were regular and consistent.

(c) communicating with residential social work colleagues to make sure they had some understanding of the work and were in agreement with it.

(d) using supervision to think through the range of activities that might be useful in helping Michael.

(e) practising the techniques in role play before the sessions.

(f) going to the workroom and familiarising myself with the materials, i.e. clay and paint. I would use this time to play and get in touch with some of the things I was feeling just before a session.

(g) using techniques of relaxation/breathing exercises, both on myself prior to sessions and with Michael in the session.

Clarity about the presenting problem and the purpose of an assessment will make it easier both to engage children and adults in the process and to help everyone make sense of the information that is collected. I once took a little girl and her brother to lunch in a solicitor's office. We explained to them what would happen in court, what the judge needed to know and what decisions he would have to make. Angela, the little girl, then put on the black gown hanging on the door and said she was going to be the judge making a decision. For the next half an hour she involved us all in enacting the court situation. Through this we learnt a great deal about Angela and her perceptions of her situation, which helped us in our assessment. She had an opportunity to express her fears and worries in a situation which she could control, and therefore begin to understand.

History-taking

To begin an assessment, we firstly need to know the history of the child in some detail. How many moves and changes of carers has the child had? What was happening to the adults at these times? What was the effect of change on the child and the adults? How did they respond? What sort of behaviour did the child show? The answer to these questions can help workers, children and those caring for them to understand more fully the problems and difficulties that the child has encountered. Roger Lake's case study of Clifford, aged five, illustrates the use of history-taking:

Clifford, aged 5½ years, is an attractive boy of black Afro-Caribbean origin. He currently lives with his mother, Yvonne, aged 25 years, and sister, Michelle, aged two years. By the time he was five, Clifford had been in care three times under Section 2, 1980 Child Care Act for relatively short periods and a variety of reasons.

Clifford's behaviour had been deteriorating over several months, according to his mother, social worker and health visitor. His mother found his frequent temper tantrums, disruptive behaviour and attention-seeking activities extremely difficult to tolerate. He was particularly difficult to control at meal and bed times, becoming aggressive and abusive towards his mother and sister. On such occasions, Yvonne had expressed the wish that he had been adopted.

The health visitor and the social worker saw the problem from a different point of view – their concern was with Yvonne's parenting. They had been worried about her difficulty in providing him with basic stimulation at home – his lack of toys and play materials, and her lack of involvement in his play. One consequence of this was a serious speech delay for which, when he was three, he had been referred for speech therapy. All these problems were a reflection of his mother's general feelings of depression and of her isolation, insecurity and lack of a permanent residence.

A previous social worker had described her as being 'sharp and impatient' with Clifford. On one occasion two years ago, a burn-mark on Clifford's arm had been reported and it was strongly felt that he was frequently hit. He was certainly a witness of extreme violence between his mother and father, a relationship which was turbulent and unhappy. His father (Leroy) spent several periods in prison for criminal offences including crimes of violence. Eventually, when Clifford was one, their relationship broke down, with Yvonne and Clifford fleeing to a Women's Aid hostel. The subsequent moves she made were ostensibly to avoid Clifford's father for fear of further violence. She had several transient relationships with men and after one such affair, Michelle, her second child was born.

Clifford's first period in care came during Yvonne's confinement with Michelle. He went home after two weeks but came back into care for a short period about a month later because Yvonne was feeling depressed and exhausted. When Clifford was five, both children were in care for a further week when Yvonne went to hospital for a termination. According to social work records, these relatively short periods in care had always been marked by Yvonne's depression, her sense of isolation, inability to cope with the demands of the children and her ambivalent feelings towards Clifford. In addition, she appeared to have a very poor self-image and was unsupported by relatives or friends.

I started working with the family shortly after Clifford's last period in care. My own contact with the family added the following information. The family were rehoused by the Council to their present address towards the end of the year prior to my beginning work with them. To her credit, Yvonne had made great efforts to use social work help to improve the quality of home life for herself and her children. Her finances and budgeting were better managed and she made use of a number of community supports – a day nursery, a mother and toddler group and the health visitor. In addition she referred herself for psychotherapy. Clifford had started school in September and reports suggested he had settled in well, his language having improved during a spell at day nursery. But throughout these improvements, his mother continued to express negative feelings towards him and complained about his behaviour.

Initial Plan for Action – the Need for Further Information

The history-taking made me realise I still had a lot to learn about Clifford before I could formulate any specific treatment goals. But Yvonne and I did agree at this point that the main identified problem was the management of Clifford's behaviour. With Yvonne's agreement, therefore, it was decided that I should make a developmental assessment of Clifford. This had not been done previously and I felt it important to ascertain how far he was behind the developmental norms for his age (Sheridan 1986). I also wanted to investigate the quality of his attachments to his mother, and his interaction with significant adults, siblings and peers (Fahlberg 1981a). In discussion with my supervisor, we anticipated that this would take three sessions. I suggested to Yvonne that when this work was completed and we had discussed it together, I might then embark on a series of direct work sessions with Clifford, and concurrently with her, help them improve the quality of their relationship.

Understanding Clifford's Development – Flow Charts and Growth Charts

My starting point was the use of a flow chart to plot the significant changes, moves and separations which had taken place in Clifford's life, (for guidance on construction of flow charts see Batty in BAAF 1984). Batty believes flow charts have two distinct purposes in child care practice:

> First, they make an excellent recording aid. A blank flow chart at the front of a file can be filled in quickly and easily as events happen, or can be 'made-up' at a time of movement or crisis more readily and for easier reference than a written report. The other purpose is less obvious and perhaps more significant. Flow charts are valuable aids to evoke feelings. An adult constructing his or her own flow chart will find him or herself experiencing again some of the feelings of joy and pain that accompanied the original events. These feelings are sometimes modified when perceived in sequence with other events on the chart as it is constructed, but as a result of the exercise, the subject's awareness of the feelings evoked in childhood is heightened. (Batty, 1984, p 50)

Yvonne sat Clifford on her knee whilst we compiled the chart. He showed little interest and was constantly distracted. He soon became bored so I changed the format we were using to an 'orange segment' as I felt he might find this easier to understand (see diagram below).

27

Born 10.1.80 in Hospital, London. Lived with Mummy at Granny's house for two days. Moved to Flat. Went to Hospital for two weeks. Tummy problem.

Daddy goes into prison. Move with Mummy to two other houses in London. Daddy hurts Mummy sometimes and they cannot live together because it makes them unhappy.

Moved to Southwark. Go into Hospital for two weeks for some tests. Start at Nursery. Move to another house a long way away at the seaside because Daddy hurt Mummy.

Move to flat in Wandsworth, go to new Nursery and meet new friends. Michelle is born. Go to 1st Foster home (Aunty Julie's). Go to 2nd Foster home (Aunty Eileen) for 1 week. Mummy not well.

Go to 3rd Foster home (A. Alison's) with Michelle for a 'holiday' because Mummy is not well. Start at Poplar Av. School. Move to new house.

Despite saying he couldn't remember early events, he spoke with excitement about his foster placements as 'holidays'. In watching this, Yvonne came to feel that he had been less affected by his brief periods in care than by witnessing the violence between herself and his father which had led to a move to the Women's Aid refuge.

In completing the 'orange', I was immediately struck by the number of moves and separations that had taken place in Clifford's life. Yvonne's presence had also helped us clarify together the tenuous and transitory relationships Yvonne established with people.

Having established details of significant events in Clifford's life, the next task was to make some assessment of Clifford's physical, cognitive and emotional development. Research from abused and neglected children suggests that this is an important initial area of investigation (Beezley, Martin and Alexander 1976). There is also a need for continuing comprehensive developmental assessments, and for social workers to be aware that many medical, behavioural and emotional problems may continue after the original abuse (Hensey et al 1983, Lynch and Roberts 1982). Significantly, Lynch and Roberts found that social workers were not always aware of the importance of medical and developmental follow-ups. They describe a case where a social worker spent considerable time talking to a mother about her relationship with her child, without seeing very much of the child, who was found by the authors to have a severe visual defect, learning difficulties and severe behaviour problems when with her peers. A similar point was made in the Beckford inquiry (Blom-Cooper 1985), which reprimanded social workers for their lack of detailed observation of children's development.

Paediatricians stress the importance of looking at children's growth and monitoring this by regular use of weight and height charts. Social workers can also make use of these tools to identify basic developmental milestones. Cooper (1986) believes that charts should be kept for all young children where there is concern about the adequacy of care. The growth curve is much more important than any single measurement. Weight height and head circumference should be checked every 2–4 weeks during the child's first year of life and every 6–12 weeks in the second and third year. Even in older children the growth curve may demonstrate periods of severe stress due to a variety of adverse environmental conditions. Social workers will always need to collaborate with medical colleagues in obtaining these details but may also find it helpful to use Sheridan's charts (1986) as indicators of normal development or delay. These illustrate the developmental progress of infants and young children up to five years old in terms of posture and large movements, vision and fine movements, hearing and speech, social behaviour and play. If there are serious areas of concern, these should be discussed with a paediatrician.

Emotional Development – Assessing Attachment and Interactions between Children and Adults

Emotional development is of primary concern to social workers. All children need secure attachments if they are to flourish and develop their potential, and it is important to get to know the details of the current and past attachment figures in a child's life. In doing so, the considerable diversity in acceptable patterns of attachment should be remembered (see Chapter 3). Quoting the work of Kennell (1976), Fahlberg describes attachment as 'an affectionate bond between two individuals that endures through time and space and serves to join them emotionally' (Fahlberg 1981a, p 7). It is widely agreed that, for the majority of children in our culture, the family provides an excellent context in which attachments may develop.

> Attachment helps the child:
> – attain his full intellectual potential
> – sort out what he perceives
> – think logically
> – develop a conscience
> – become self-reliant
> – cope with stress and frustration
> – handle fear and worry
> – develop future relationships
> – reduce jealousy. (Fahlberg 1981a, p 7)

In assessing attachment, social workers should make detailed observations of children and their interaction with the adults responsible for their care. It should be remembered that the function of attachment is protection. The primary carers provide a secure base from which children can explore, and to which they can return, especially should they become tired or frightened. Their behaviour complements children's attachment behaviour (Bowlby 1986) and it is important to look at the sensitivity of parents or carers to a child's overtures, their awareness of children as individuals, their interactions with their children and how they set limits and discipline them.

Many children who come into care may have experienced their parents as unpredictable, inconsistent, unresponsive, insensitive or rejecting (Bretherton and Waters 1985). This may create a pattern of attachment behaviour in the children which then makes it difficult for adult carers to respond to their needs. The issue of whether early attachments irrevocably influence a child's later capacity to make affectionate bonds is contentious (see Chapter 3). There is, however, no doubt that childhood experiences can influence many factors in adulthood, particularly the pattern and stability of relationships (Rutter 1981 and 1985, Quinton and Rutter 1984). Recent evidence also indicates that changes in attachment patterns can occur through emotionally corrective experiences in relationships (see Chapter 5). These changes can be a result of:

1 a change in the pattern of the early relationships through time
2 through repeated experiences in other relationships that break the pattern of earlier experiences
3 through an especially strong emotional experience within a single relationship that breaks the pattern of earlier experiences.

It is clearly an important task for social workers both to assess the nature and quality of a child's attachments and then to seek to provide the kinds of experience that help to facilitate change.

Children's Personalities and their Reactions to their Experiences

Attachment is only one aspect of children's emotional development. We also need to find out how children have reacted to other important experiences (Beezley et al 1976). We must understand the nature of their peer relationships, their relationships with other significant adults, such as teachers, their schooling, their interests and their cultural and racial experiences.

In a follow-up study of 50 abused children, Martin and Beezley (1977) found that over half had poor self-images, were sorrowful children and acted in a manner which was upsetting to their parents, teachers and peers. Some were withdrawn, others were difficult and defiant. Certain characteristics could be noted with disturbing frequency:

- impaired ability for enjoyment
- behavioural adjustment symptoms
- low self-esteem
- withdrawal
- opposition
- hyper-vigilance
- compulsivity
- pseudo-adult behaviour.

Throughout all of what has been said above, it is important to remember that children's development is the result of the interactions between them, their family and their environment. Problems in any one of these areas can interrupt the normal process of growth and change.

Roger Lake used the developmental charts in conjunction with check-lists of attachments in three sessions with Clifford and his mother. They helped to emphasise the relationship between his development and the quality of his attachment to his mother. In the first two sessions, Roger asked Clifford to complete simple tasks such as copying a triangle and a square and identifying colours, and in so doing Roger was able to observe Clifford's vision and fine movements. Similarly, using Sheridan's guidance on large movements, he asked Clifford to run, jump and dance to music. These activities were performed willingly and with enthusiasm, particularly the dancing (information which Roger was to use later in his direct work sessions). Clifford's speech was studied and his memory tested. He knew his name but found it difficult to remember his address, which was perhaps not surprising as they had recently moved. He understood times of day but, like many five-year-olds, had difficulty with clock time. Overall, it was clear that Clifford was easily able to accomplish the majority of tasks set.

Roger Lake also involved Clifford's mother in the process, by affirming her value as an information giver:

> In relation to his social behaviour and play, Yvonne had informed me, and I had already observed, that he is usually well able to use a knife and fork, cannot wash his own face but can dress or undress himself, although he often gets muddled with buttons. Yvonne also said that she thought his behaviour had been getting generally worse, particularly at meal times and bedtimes.

Out of these sessions Roger was struck by two significant factors, firstly Yvonne's lack of encouragement for Clifford during the tasks; she found some of his efforts amusing, appearing to laugh at him in a mocking way. Secondly, he was struck by the tentative way in which Clifford approached the tasks. Roger felt Clifford was going to need regular encouragement and praise at appropriate times during any play sessions.

Roger comments:

> For the next session, I wanted to make my own observations of Clifford's behaviour and his relationship with his mother, so I

deliberately did a home visit at a meal time, identified by Yvonne as being 'difficult'. Not for the first time, the house was full of Yvonne's friends. Despite the chaotic atmosphere, we managed to spend time with Clifford in the kitchen, before and after his supper. Clifford was in a tetchy mood, unable to settle at the table, hurling cutlery around, and shouting that he wanted to watch TV. Despite his remonstrations, he eventually ate his food with little fuss.

Using Fahlberg's checklist on attachment (1981a), I noted several problems in Clifford's behaviour. He made defiant responses to his mother's requests, characterised by 'No, I won't', or 'Do it yourself'. He seemed most preoccupied by television, often displayed in-appropriate reactions in the presence of adults and appeared 'too familiar' and sophisticated in their presence. He expressed frustra-tion by shouting, being physically aggressive or excessively moody. He did respond well to physical affection from his mother when sitting on her knee or when given a cuddle, but the overtures were not particularly spontaneous.

I observed that the measures to discipline Clifford were inconsis-tent and dependent on his mother's moods. 'Bedroom' was a punishment, as was 'smacking'. A positive fact was that Yvonne was able to show some interest in his development, commenting on his rate of growth and how his speech had improved since starting school. Although there did appear to be signs of a genuine affectionate relationship between them (she often spoke of how she loved him, and there were cuddles), Yvonne spoke of how Clifford's physical appearance and behaviour had reminded her so much of his father that she sometimes had nightmares that he was 'mad, just like his father'.

Finally, I checked out details of Clifford's functioning with his school teacher, since he spent a significant part of his day at school. Here, he was described as 'a rather isolated and independent little boy who had difficulty in making friends, often having fights'. (This was in contrast to Clifford's own version, which was that he had 'lots of friends at school'.)

Putting the Assessment Together

From being with Clifford and talking to his mother, observing them together and constructing flow charts and developmental charts, Roger had learned a good deal about Clifford's functioning, his interaction with his mother, his physical and emotional development and the impact of his past separations and moves. Roger's assessment was as follows:

1 Clifford's mother had difficulty in relating his behaviour to his past experiences or her mixed feelings towards him. Sadly, she did not have the parenting skills to understand his need to explore his own world through his imagination or play, and had not been able to enjoy him as a child.
2 These feelings, coupled with the numerous separations in his early life, had contributed to his shaky sense of trust in his mother, and had blunted his confidence.
3 There had been a deterioration in Clifford's behaviour both at home and at school and a worsening of the relationship between Clifford and his mother so that their interaction was in danger of becoming a downward spiral leading to family breakdown. The more Clifford behaved badly, the more his mother was likely to reject him.
4 Weighing the pros and cons of Clifford's development and his relationship with his mother, there were pointers to potential for change, such as warmth between them and concern from Yvonne about his progresss. A critical factor was that any positive responses from Clifford would be dependent upon his mother initiating positive interaction with him, thus promoting his self-worth and self-esteem.

Formulating Goals

This assessment led Roger Lake to formulate goals and a treatment plan which would take approximately three to four months. The overall goal, within the context of permanency planning, was to prevent family breakdown. To achieve this, Roger proposed a treatment plan on two levels. Firstly, there would be six direct work sessions with Clifford, aimed at helping him sort out his confusion about the past, and build up his sense of self-wealth by learning to play as a five-year-old. Secondly, these sessions would be followed by work with Yvonne to increase her understanding of Clifford's behavioural problems and help her change her own behaviour towards him. This might be achieved by direct one-to-one work, family therapy and linking her to community supports such as a family centre, or providing her with a family aid.

In involving both Clifford and his mother in the programme, Roger Lake recognized the danger that workers can become so involved in direct work with children that adults caring for them feel jealous and excluded and children's permanent relationships may be placed in jeopardy. The worker's task is not to become a substitute parent. Peter Daniel and Andrew Small both found this to be critical to the success of their work (see Chapters 4 and 10). Fahlberg's three publications (1981a, 1981b and 1982) provide a helpful discussion of these issues.

Outcome

Assessment and treatment go hand in hand. Space precludes a detailed discussion of the treatment plan for Clifford and his mother. Roger Lake had to prepare for his direct sessions with Clifford, working out the techniques and materials which he would use. During the sessions he learned more about Clifford's problems and potential. He recognised that assessment was ongoing throughout his intervention. Sometimes, information about the child's problems can only be discovered when a child feels confident enough to trust an adult. You can only assess the potential for resolving problems by providing a context in which progress can be made. So it was with Clifford. By giving him the time, space and opportunities for therapeutic play, Clifford's behaviour began to improve, which, in turn, provoked a more positive response from the adults around him. This was only a beginning, but enough change had occurred in Clifford's behaviour to confirm that the original assessment had been correct in predicting potential for change. The direct work sessions revealed that more work would have to be done with Clifford and his family to consolidate his progress.

Roger Lake was about to begin his planned work with Clifford's mother when another crisis occurred: 'Yvonne rang me to say she had left her home and was in a Women's Aid hostel with the children. Leroy was pursuing her – and she had fled in fear. I realized there was still much work to be done'. A new phase of assessment and treatment was about to begin.

3 Work with Children Experiencing Separation and Loss: A Theoretical Framework *Jane Aldgate*

The concepts of separation and loss are very much part of the everyday vocabulary of social work. Loss may take many forms (Marris 1974), but recognizing the common elements of different events enhances our understanding of individuals' reactions to them. Loss can have a liberating outcome for adults, bringing relief from prolonged stress. Adverse experiences such as early loss can increase the coping capacity of some individuals (Rutter 1981) but, for many children, unwilling separation from significant adults will be a frightening event. Children will react in many ways according to their age, prior experiences and stage of development. An important mediating factor may be the way in which separation is handled. Another important factor is outcome. Where separations lead to considerable adversity for children this may have more damaging effects than the separation itself.

In child care social work, attention must be paid to separations which are the result of the movement of children in and out of care. Stevenson summarizes the impact of admission to care on children. During this event, 'We are breaking prematurely the lifeline of the developing child' (Stevenson 1968, p 9). The same could be said of moves in care where attachments have been made, or of children's return to their birth families. What is the significance of this break? What are the consequences of separation for children in the short- and the long-term? Is it important that a child's lifeline is repaired, and if so, what part can social workers play in this? This chapter attempts to address these questions, to provide reassurance for workers and some ideas about where to begin. It makes no attempt to be comprehensive, but selects literature and research which social workers may find useful in analysing the meaning of separation and loss for the children with whom they are working.

Background: Child Development and Attachment Theory

It is difficult to comprehend the impact of separation on any child without a knowledge of both child development and attachment theory. Understanding the diversities of both normal and abnormal attachment is an essential part of assessing children, as Margaret Adcock describes in Chapter 2. What is particularly relevant to experiences of separation and loss is the recognition that children are resilient to change and have the potential to adapt to different patterns of attachment.

It used to be thought that there was 'a critical period' for the development of attachment between babies and mothers. If this did not take place, it was argued, a child's development would be seriously affected. Where separation took place in early childhood, it was likely that the effects of this would be long-lasting. While it is obviously advantageous if early, secure attachments can be established between children and their carers, it does not necessarily follow that if children are subsequently separated from their primary attachment figures they will be irreversibly damaged. Recent research by Herbert et al (1982) refutes the notion of 'a sensitive period' in the formation of mother-to-infant attachment. If this were so, they argue, the adoption of small babies, let alone older children, would be necessarily unsuccessful. Attachment is not a mechanical, all-or-nothing phenomenon, but a complicated process, subject to later modification (see Chapter 5).

Additionally, current thinking suggests that there is room in our multi-cultural society for a variety of acceptable patterns of attachment between young children and their families (Clarke and Clarke 1976). Although it is common, even with small children, for there to be a hierarchy of attachment, with certain adults taking on more importance than others, research indicates that infants are capable of making deep attachments to several significant people (Schaffer and Emerson 1964, Schaffer 1977). Sylva and Lunt summarize the current thinking:

> There is no scientific foundation for the myth of the blood bond or the belief that the biological mother alone is uniquely capable of caring for her child. This loving relationship may be carried out or shared by one or several other adults provided that they show certain qualities. What are these qualities? Sensitivity, consistency, stimulation and responsiveness are some of the qualities important to the early relationship in a young child's life. (Sylva and Lunt 1982, pp 50–51)

Clearly, what is significant to children's development is the *quality* of the care offered.

37

Understanding the diversities of attachment and the quality of an individual child's experiences are necessary prerequisites for helping children through experiences of separation and loss. As Margaret Adcock suggests in Chapter 2, attachment is part of a protection mechanism. It therefore follows that separating children from attachment figures is likely to engender in them acute fear. The most frightening thing for children is to be simultaneously afraid *and* separated from their attachment figures. This, Fahlberg (1981a) suggests, is what makes moves in care so frightening. It also explains why some children who have been abused by their parents may be reluctant to separate from them. In separation, the reactions of these children may be so tentative, because they fear reprisals, that they are often in danger of being overlooked in the midst of admission-to-care activity (Black 1984). Bowlby makes a useful comparison between a child's anxiety over unwanted separation from an attachment figure to 'the anxiety that the General of an expeditionary force feels when communications with his base are cut or threatened' (Bowlby 1986, p 62). Seeing separation in this way, as a legitimate cause of fear, also defines the social worker's role – to help children express their feelings and come to terms with their separation. Before we discuss the social worker's role in detail, let us look at the range of reactions which children may display and some of the factors which will influence those reactions.

Children's Immediate Reactions to Separation and Loss

Anxiety and fear are emotions which many children will experience when separated from adults to whom they are attached, but are only the first part of the process of reaction – which has been well documented (see for example, Fahlberg 1981b, Jewett 1984, and Kubler-Ross 1972). This process may also include some or all of the following emotions: shock, alarm, denial and disbelief, yearning and pining, searching, anger or guilt, disorganization, despair and, finally, reorganization and integration. Children may go through some or all of these stages, but not necessarily in the order given. Their experiences of attachment will have a primary influence on their reactions to separation but there are other factors which may determine the way in which they respond, including cultural expectations, age, gender, temperament, cognitive appraisal and 'set', and social circumstances before and after separation.

Cultural Expectations

Cultural reactions to separation and loss may be significant in determining a child's ability to resolve his or her feelings (Kaffman and Elizir 1983). Jewett (1984) and Black (1984) argue that one major problem for children in Western cultures is the denial of mourning rituals. It is also well known that the loss of cultural reference points may cause very special problems for immigrants (Cheetham 1972, Lim 1983), while Small (1986) has drawn attention to the problems of identity confusion which some black children may have when living in transracial placements or in children's homes where all the staff are white.

Age of Children at Separation

Age is a major factor affecting children's responses to loss. A child's perception and understanding of death, for example, may vary with age and related cognitive ability (Orbach et al 1985). Reactions will also vary with age; Black (1984), for example, found that one year after bereavement, younger children tended to show aggressive symptoms while the older ones showed sadness and depression.

Secondly, age may act as a protective factor against stress in young children (Rutter 1981). Even though very young babies may sense changes around them (Fahlberg 1982), it is likely that 'children below the age of six or seven months are relatively immune because they have not yet developed selective attachments and therefore are not able to experience separation and anxiety' (Rutter 1981, p 337).

Children of above school age may also be protected to some extent because advantage may be taken of 'an older child's ability to understand situations and develop strategies for dealing with them' (Rutter 1985, p 606). Research into children admitted to hospital (Stacey et al 1970) has shown that older children have the cognitive skills to appreciate that separation 'does not necessarily mean abandonment or loss of a relationship and to understand better what is involved in hospitalization and why unpleasant medical or surgical procedures may be necessary' (Rutter 1981, p 337).

Children between six and 33 months are least likely to be protected by their age (Benians 1982). In this age group, children do not have the cognitive ability to make total sense of what is happening to them, and the younger child may find it difficult to hold attachment figures in

39

mind for the duration of a separation or to understand the nature of death (Rutter 1981 and 1985). These young children need special attention when coming into care to ensure that they are placed with families who can offer them a *consistent* experience. Any parental visits should occur daily to avoid detachment (Cooper 1986).

Gender

One area which sometimes receives little attention is that of gender difference. Overall, boys appear to be more vulnerable to the effects of separation than girls (Rutter 1981, Wallerstein and Kelly 1980 and Hetherington 1980). The reasons for this are so far unclear, but given that boys seem more vulnerable to behavioural disturbances while in care (Rowe and Lambert 1973), this may be an important factor to bear in mind when working with children in separation.

Temperamental Characteristics

Children are individuals with different temperaments and different personalities. Research into child abuse had suggested that a child's temperament may affect the way adults respond to him or her (Lynch 1975). So, in separation, children's temperamental responses may well influence the way they are perceived and responded to by adults. Research in this area is still at an early stage (Rutter 1972, 1981), but given that temperament is often accounted for as a variable in the linking of children and foster or adoptive families (Aldgate and Hawley 1986 and Tizard 1977), it should not be dismissed.

Cognitive Appraisal and Set

Alongside temperament, there are two important individual attributes which may influence the outcome of a separation experience: cognitive appraisal and 'cognitive set' (Rutter 1981 and 1985).

There are two main points to be borne in mind here. Firstly, reactions will depend on perceptions of the event – or 'cognitive appraisal'. Separation or loss may be seen as either positive or threatening; a change of school may be anticipated by one child with pleasure and by another with terror. Stacey et al (1970) found that children who were accustomed to brief, happy separations from parents, during time spent with grandparents for example, tended to react better to hospital admissions than children who had never experienced separation from their primary attachment figures. Cognitive appraisal may be influenced by the intervention of adults – parents, carers or social workers – in preparing children for impending changes.

Secondly, allied to cognitive appraisal of an event is a child's 'cognitive set'. This is best defined as 'a sense of self-esteem and self-efficacy which makes successful coping more likely'. The corollary of this is 'a sense of helplessness which increases the likelihood that one adversity will lead to another' (Rutter 1985, p 603). Rutter's views have much in common with conclusions drawn from work done on the relationship between the identity and the well-being of children in care (Weinstein 1960, Colón, 1973, Thorpe 1980). It is a consideration which warrants urgent attention when dealing with black children in care, who may, through exposure to institutionalized racism, be encouraged to deny their positive racial identity (see Chapter 6, and Maximé 1986, Small 1986).

Naturally, the children most likely to develop a positive 'cognitive set' are those who, within the context of their own culture and community, have been exposed to 'secure, stable, affectional relationships, and experiences of success and achievement' (Rutter 1985, p 607). Recent work (Quinton et al 1984, Rutter and Quinton 1984) suggests, however, that success and achievement do not need to be general. Even where parents have been unable to provide an environment to facilitate optimal child development, children may find compensation in success at school or in sports or in relationships with other adults. Furthermore, compensatory experiences of success and achievement may be retained to enable an individual to cope in adult life. These new lines of research have major implications for social work with children experiencing separation and loss. They urge us to move away from a problem-focussed intervention to one which identifies strengths and coping mechanisms, drawing evidence from all of a child's social and developmental activities. Such an approach demands a sophisticated understanding of cultural, ethnic and racial differences (see Chapter 6).

Futhermore, the potential influence of 'cognitive set' adds weight to the permanency planning movement. Children who move from place to place may well lose a sense of control over their lives and develop 'learned helplessness' (Seligman 1975). It also adds credibility to the legislation that permits children's wishes and feelings to be taken into account in making decisions about their future (Child Care Act 1980).

41

It is well known that school-aged children are likely to blame themselves for an untimely separation. Appropriate involvement of children in the analysis of why, for example, a foster placement may have failed will help them place their part in the event in perspective. Disruption meetings (see Fitzgerald 1983) are now commonly held in social work agencies. These should offer older children the opportunity to present their views. After all, the process of negotiation between parents and children in many families, irrespective of class, ethnicity or race, is one way in which children gain the confidence to assert themselves, and at the same time learn to accept appropriate boundaries set by adults. Self-control is as much a part of learning to achieve as is praise for success.

Reasons for Separation

A final factor likely to influence a child's reactions to separation, linked to 'cognitive set', is the environment in which he or she had been living before the separation occurred. The exposure over a long period of time to a multiplicity of disadvantages, including poverty, persistent tension and disharmonious relationships with and between parents or carers, is likely to take its toll on a child's coping abilities. It is this association with unsatisfactory family relationships, rather than loss itself, which 'may serve to sensitize and increase vulnerability to later losses' (Rutter 1981, p 349). In other words, the reasons for separation may have more effect on children in the long term than the separation itself.

Clearly, it is very important that special attention be paid to such children at the point of entry to care, to provide them with maximum stability and protect them from further disadvantage.

What Happens After Separation

An understanding of the circumstances prior to separation, and a knowledge of the various factors which may affect children's reactions, are essential parts of a social work assessment aiming to make the best possible plans for children and their families. It is also essential to know which circumstances are most likely to promote children's recovery. First and foremost, stability and quality in relationships with adults is a crucial factor, as a comparison of post-separation circumstances drawn from research studies suggests. Even young children who seem distressed may recover from short separations when returned to a family who can continue to meet their developmental needs (Heinike and Westheimer 1965, Rutter 1981). Additionally, although many children show behaviour problems following bereavement or divorce, the recovery rate from these problems is also high (Black 1984). A major factor which will affect recovery is family functioning. The psychological and physical health of parents and the relationship between parents, and parents and children, will affect the outcome for the child (Rutter 1981, Richards and Dyson 1982). Children are least likely to recover when, after a separation, they return to families where multiple long-standing psycho-social problems are still in existence. If children remain separated from their families in care, they are likely to be most disadvantaged if they experience multiple carers and little stability (Keane 1983, Wolkind and Rutter 1973, Rowe and Lambert 1973, Thorpe 1980). In extreme circumstances, some of these experiences may predispose children who have grown up in care to become poor parents themselves (Quinton and Rutter 1984). The most devastating effects for any child are likely to occur when separation or loss is part of 'a chain of adversity' (Sylva and Lunt, p 37). Here no one factor, including the separation itself, is responsible for damaging a child, but circumstances before, during and after separation contribute to the child's disadvantage.

Social Work Intervention in Mediating the Effects of Separation and Loss – Some Guidelines for Practice

While many children may make a spontaneous recovery from experiences of separation or loss, many of those who come into contact with social workers are likely to have had some experience of disadvantage. The primary responsibility of the social worker is to ensure that coming into care does not contribute to the 'chain of adversity'. Priority must be given to permanency planning. To this end, workers have a legitimate role in providing both psychological and practical help to children and families at this time. It is, however, important that social workers recognize the boundaries of their work. If they are dealing with children and families whose pathology is beyond the bounds of normal stress reactions, it is essential to seek help from other professionals who have greater competence in these areas.

1 A Crisis Intervention Approach

A good starting point is the principle that any social work intervention designed to effect mediation of the negative effects of separation and loss must be based on a fundamental belief that separation involves fear which needs to be mastered, and that loss involves grief which needs to be expressed. Separation or loss will place children under stress. The long-term outcome of coping with this stress may depend on how it is handled at the time and whether the result is a point of growth – or failure (Rutter 1981). Winnicott goes so far as to assert that 'if we could only learn to respond effectively to children at the crisis point in their lives which brings them to us, and at subsequent crisis points which are a part of growth, we may save many of them from becoming clients in one capacity or another for the rest of their lives' (Winnicott 1986, p 38).

Although this extreme view might give the mistaken impression that all children's problems associated with separation experiences can be solved by social work intervention, it nevertheless reaffirms the point that separation or loss is a significant event, warranting a carefully considered response. Whether workers tackle intervention alone or in collaboration with others is a matter of professional judgement. The goal is to provide the best, carefully timed, appropriate intervention for children.

Within the bounds of a worker's competence and skills, there is no one social work method which is completely appropriate for working with children who are facing separation and loss. Sometimes, the task may be to change children's behaviour in preparation for separation (Hudson and Macdonald 1986). At other times, bereavement counselling, which involves either reflective or activity-based ways of working, may be more appropriate (Black 1984). Where separation or loss occurs suddenly, a crisis intervention approach is likely to be the most helpful. 'Crisis' is one of the most misused words in everyday social work language, but one writer who makes a sensible and relevant application of 'crisis theory' to child care practice is Donley. In her work on disruption, she describes the value of responding promptly to situations, without panic. Her advice could be widely applied to many situations involving separation and loss:

> Slow down, broadly assess the situation, seek advice, eliminate any impulses to assigning blame, examine the capabilities of the child and family, negotiate an agreeable plan of action. (Donley 1978, p 77)

2 Involving Significant Adults

Helping children through separation cannot be accomplished without accounting for the adults who hold significant places in their lives. The involvement of these adults will vary according to the nature of the loss and their own coping abilities. Sometimes parents and children share a common grief. Recognizing this, work on bereavement or divorce has recommended a family therapy approach (Bentovim 1982, Black 1984). The same approach is very appropriate for children who are separating from foster or adoptive families (Fitzgerald 1983, Aldgate and Hawley 1986).

Children will also benefit from trusted adults helping to prepare them for separation and loss (see for example, Fahlberg 1981b, Kline and Overstreet 1972, Jewett 1984, Aldgate and Hawley 1986). The value of parental presence at admission to care, to reassure children that they have not been abandoned (Aldgate 1980, Millham et al 1985), or at admission to hospital (Stacey et al 1970), has been convincingly demonstrated by researchers.

Before adults can properly help their children to face separation or loss, they may need intervention in their own right at this time of crisis. Studies of the separation experiences of parents at admission to care (Jenkins and Norman 1972, Aldgate 1976), and on the devastating effects of disruption on foster families (Aldgate and Hawley 1986), demonstrate the value of this approach, while Whittaker (1981), Gambrill and Stein (1981) and Maluccio et al (1986) provide practical examples of how work may be accomplished.

3 Work with Children

Children also need help in their own right at this time. The process of intervention is described more fully in Chapter 10, but its essential features are as follows:
- preparation for separation
- honesty from workers about the need for separation or why loss has occurred
- giving children permission and the opportunity to express their feelings to protect them from later emotional cut-offs
- preserving continuity with the past, preferably by maintaining links with kin.

Readers may like to consult the following studies for detailed guidance on direct work with children facing separation or loss: Jewett (1984), Fahlberg (1981a, 1981b) and Fitzgerald (1983).

4 Separations and Permanency Planning

Every separation is a discrete and important event in itself, but should also be seen as an opportunity for significant social work which will contribute to the general long-term welfare of the child: in short, any separation, especially one which occurs in an emergency, should be seen in the context of permanency planning. It is irrelevant whether the plan is for a child to live at home, be rehabilitated, enter a shared care arrangement or be transferred to a permanent alternative family. The creation of an environment which will promote enduring attachments and a positive sense of identity and self-esteem is paramount.

Given the diversity of the backgrounds of children coming into care and the complexities involved in linking children to alternative families, it would be unrealistic to deny that in some cases permanency planning may involve a dynamic aspect: it may not be possible to get it right first time round. Parker (1985) sensibly suggests that all workers should make contingency plans for children who come into care, in case a placement breaks down. If it does, Donley urges us to see this event as 'an interruption in the process leading to a long-term goal' (Fitzgerald 1983, p 6), to guard against feelings of failure, and to avoid workers blaming themselves – or carers or parents. The idea that a disruption may be 'almost a dress rehearsal for the real thing' (Donley 1978, p 38) then shifts the emphasis from a success/failure dichotomy to seeing what can be learned from a separation and how it may be turned into a positive experience for all concerned.

5 What Social Workers Can Do to Prepare Themselves

Working with children and families who are experiencing separation places considerable demands on social workers but there are certain things which they can do to prepare themselves for the task in hand. The first guiding principle is that work with children is no different from work with adults, and must be set within the context of a professional relationship.

Children in their everyday lives are used to contact with adults who are there for a specific purpose – playgroup leaders, teachers, child-minders, doctors. Even very young children have a rudimentary understanding of the different roles which adults play in their lives. The qualities which children often admire in these adults are kindness and firmness. Young children appreciate teachers who have a natural sense of authority, provide clear boundaries and yet can demonstrate a partiality towards them as individuals. It is the same with social workers: children will see them for what they are as individuals, but they are also quite capable of recognizing the role of social worker as long as this is made clear. The fact that the social worker's task often involves touching deep emotional areas when working with children makes it difficult to preserve the boundaries of the relationship. It is essential that we do, for if we do not, 'if we side-step the professional nature of our work and mislead children into thinking that we are available indefinitely as their best friend, we are badly letting them down' (Winnicott 1986, p 47). Margaret Adcock explores these concepts further in Chapter 10, with reference to the successful ending of relationships.

Being professional does not mean denying empathy (Winnicott 1986). This discipline can only be achieved by developing great self-awareness. Because experiences of loss are universal, seeing children in distress may evoke recollections of workers' own experiences. Some of these may not have been resolved; they may get in the way of work with the child unless they are confronted and examined in supervision (see Chapter 8). Fitzgerald, talking about separation resulting from disruption of placements, urges workers to ask themselves, 'Am I having too much pain at the thought of disruption even to listen?' (Fitzgerald 1983, p 40). Pain may not only stem from the worker's own memories of separation, it will also involve a complex mixture of emotions, including anger towards the adults who are seen to have put the child in this predicament, and guilt about the inadequacy of resources or the breakdown of a family placement in which there has been a high investment of time and energy. Furthermore, there may be an overwhelming desire to protect children from exposure to pain by avoiding the subject of separation (Maluccio et al, 1986). Nonetheless, the grieving process must be allowed to take place. The child must be comforted but the tears must not be stopped (Stevenson 1968).

The task of helping children through separation and loss is made all the more difficult in Social Service Departments by the fact that it is part of a wider context of work. At admission to care, or at a change of placement, the social worker not only has the role of offering direct help to children but also of working with significant adults. The worker is a resource-finder, a negotiator and, in some cases, where children are being compulsorily removed from their parents, an authority figure; all these activities must be accomplished in a very short space of time, by working at an intensive pace. The work demands a great deal of physical and emotional energy. Workers will often find themselves dealing with deeply-felt emotions, both within themselves and within their clients. Sometimes, the complexity of the intervention legitimately demands separate workers for parents and children. Whatever model of service delivery is adopted, it is essential that problems are shared and that workers avail themselves of adequate support so that the goal of intervention may be accomplished – to help a child 'get ready for the future with increasingly diminishing concern for the past' (Jewett 1984, p 130).

4 Aspects of work with emotionally damaged children *Jane Aldgate and John Simmonds with Peter Daniel, Gail Martin and Venetia Pigott*

Many children are vulnerable to emotional damage (Kellmer Pringle 1975). The causes are complex but may include long-standing psycho-social family adversity, inconsistency or inadequacy in parenting, impaired attachment, lack of resolution of major crises in childhood such as separation from parents or multiple changes of parents, carers and residences, to name but a few. As suggested in Chapter 3, it is often the interrelationship between several factors which causes most damage to a child, rather than one stressful event.

There are two main concepts which are useful for workers to consider in relation to emotional damage in children. The first is *privation*, where children have lacked any opportunity to form affectional bonds (Rutter 1972). Many early studies of children brought up in institutions provided searing evidence of the consequences of privation (see Dinnage and Kellmer Pringle 1967). The second concept is *deprivation* – where children have experienced some early affectional bonds, but where these have been disrupted and not satisfactorily replaced by others. The worst outcome seems to be where children have experienced multiple carers or have been subject to the chain of adversity described in the previous chapter.

Research suggests that deprivation can be reversed, either wholly or partially (see Chapter 5), but that privation is more difficult to counteract in later life (Rutter 1972), although there have been clinical accounts of partial recovery from extreme early privation (Skuse 1984).

This chapter looks at three young people who experienced emotional deprivation as a result of separations earlier in their lives, with the consequence that they had gaps in their development which made it difficult for them to make transitions, in one case from one foster home to another, and in the second, from a disrupted adoptive home to a foster home. In the third case, turning a foster home into an adoptive home presented the problem.

In the course of normal child development, children pass through a complex process in order to reach 'integration' – the development of a stable sense of self. Dockar-Drysdale, whose therapeutic work with children at the Mulberry Bush School is legendary, elaborates further on this concept. To achieve integration children have to go through stages of:

> Experience, realization, symbolization and conceptualization. By this I mean quite simply that a child may have a good experience provided by his therapist, but that this will be of no value to him until he is able, eventually, to realise it, that is to say to feel that this good thing has really happened to him. Then he must find a way of storing the good thing inside him, which he does by means of symbolizing the experience. Last in the series of processes comes conceptualization, which is understanding intellectually what has happened to him in the course of the experience, and being able to think this in words: conceptualization is only of value if it is retrospective – ideas must be the sequel to experience. (Dockar-Drysdale 1968, p 82)

Some children with gaps in their development may appear to be 'stuck' at an earlier chronological age. Fahlberg divides the way children can become 'stuck' into four areas:

- developmental delays in any or all of the three major areas – physical, cognitive and psychological.
- the child may have developed abnormal patterns of behaviour – maladaptive patterns.
- unresolved separation issues may cause the child to become stuck.
- misperceptions can hinder the usual progression of growth and change. (Fahlberg 1984, p 17)

The social worker's task is to help children close the gaps, put together the missing bits of the past and make sufficient sense of them to allow integration to occur, enabling them to relate to others in a realistic and positive way. There are many approaches to this and practitioners will need to find those which both suit them and are appropriate to the child they are working with. In the work described below, Gail Martin, Peter Daniel and Venetia Pigott show how an enabling relationship and well established techniques, including flow charts (see Chapter 2), play (see Chapter 9), the compilation of a life story book and a child 'ecomap', can be adapted to meet the needs of individual children.

Fahlberg (1981b) sees the life story book as 'an opportunity to identify strong feelings about past events, to resolve issues, to correct misperceptions'. The life book can help:

1. to organise past events in the chronological schema;
2. to aid in ego development;
3. to increase self-esteem;
4. a child re-read at his own pace;
5. a child share in orderly fashion his past with selected others;
6. build a sense of trust for the worker who aids in compiling the book;
7. gain acceptance of all facets of the child's life and help the child accept his own past; and
8. facilitate bonding. (Fahlberg 1981b, p 52)

The 'ecomap' was also developed by Fahlberg (1981b). Describing her work, Ryan and Walker say,

> This was originally developed as an initial interviewing tool to open communication between the child and social worker. It shows the child and various people, places and concerns which form a part of his or her life. Children can discuss these elements and how they relate to them and so gain further understanding of their life as a whole and why they are where they are. (Ryan and Walker 1985, p 32)

Further guidance on these techniques and others can be sought from Lightbown 1979, Fahlberg 1981b, BAAF 1984, Ryan and Walker 1985, Owen and Curtis 1983.

Translating the Theory into Practice

Any social work intervention with children whose emotional development has been damaged or delayed must be based on sound assessment along the lines suggested in Chapter 2. Having made the assessment, work can begin. Sometimes, the initial problem for the worker is to overcome passive resistance in children. This calls for perseverance, as Gail Martin found in her work with Patrick.

Patrick

Patrick, at eleven and in care for the past nine years, had experienced much of the inconsistency and discontinuity which still too often characterize long-term care. He had been living with his present foster parents for four years, although the placement was by no means legally and emotionally secure. Patrick was showing many of the signs of an emotionally damaged child: intellectual and emotional immaturity, poor impulse control and low self-esteem. While his needs were extensive, Gail Martin suggested, as a starting point, that they construct a life story book together. Patrick was as much interested in the meals that accompanied the trips to find out information as the information itself, but they both persevered until they started to do some work on the previous foster placement.

> When we reached this point in the life story book, Patrick suggested that we really didn't need to include it, we should miss out these two years. I pursued the subject gently and tried, as in the past, to explain that grown-ups sometimes cannot cope when things go wrong as they had in that family. We considered some of the photographs from that period and then on some scrap paper Patrick did a drawing. He pointed out that it was a lock surrounded by a door with a room behind it, the room in which the foster mother locked him when he was naughty. Patrick never before had been this specific about his memories of those days. I wondered if he might like to repeat the drawing in his life story book, a suggestion he took up readily. He then wrote a description of the drawing telling what had happened to him and how much he hated being locked in. He added his strong negative feelings about the foster mother.

It was clear that Patrick's feelings about his foster placement were very strong and something he had previously felt unable to express. While extreme care should be given to applying interpretation to a child's drawing (see Oaklander 1978), in this case Patrick's drawing did seem to be related to an actual experience. Gail adds,

> This was the first time the subject had been discussed on Patrick's terms and he had not felt the need to hide from it. Distressing as his experiences had been, he was no longer overwhelmed by them. At our next meeting, a planned outing with his brother, Patrick asked whether next time we could do more work on his book. After my initial shock it occurred to me that, in expressing his feelings about his foster placement, Patrick had freed himself of his reluctance to look at the past . . . it seemed as though at last he could begin to rid himself of some of the blame for these disastrous events.

Patrick was beginning to come to terms with the past, and the future looked promising. Venetia Pigott's work with Richard was more difficult because, as Venetia writes, 'He had to come to terms with the multiplicity of attachments, losses, separations and rejections, and the fear and anxiety that the process of resolution would involve.' Venetia

Pigott stressed the importance of her relationship with Richard in facilitating the helping process: 'My intention, to paraphrase Mattinson (1975), was less a matter of applying a technique than forming a relationship'.

Richard

Richard was born when his mother was 16 and still at school. Pressure from his maternal grandmother compelled his parents to marry despite their young age. His father was a petty criminal whose spells in prison left his wife and baby son unsupported both financially and emotionally. His mother wished to continue her studies, and Richard was left with a series of carers, including his maternal grandmother. Eventually, the strain became too great, and when he was two, Richard was received into care. He was placed in a children's home where one of his carers, Mrs Hopkins, describes how Richard initially lay for hours in his cot staring at the ceiling and avoiding eye contact. His cognitive, motor and intellectual development was severely retarded; he could not speak, and showed little signs of beginning to play. He was thought to be subnormal, although, when seen by an educational psychologist 18 months later, he was described as a very intelligent little boy.

Fortunately for Richard, he received sensitive and informed care of a high quality from the residential staff. He was the youngest in the children's home and was made much of by the staff and other children. Mrs Hopkins and one other member of staff cared for Richard exclusively, recognising the vital importance of continuity and consistency. They gave him as much physical and intellectual stimulation as was possible.

Richard was placed with his adoptive parents when he was three years old. He continued to live with his new family until they separated, when he was eight, leaving Richard with his adoptive mother. He was sent to a boarding school when he was nine, and to a school for 'maladjusted' children when he was ten. After several unsettled years, his relationship with his adoptive mother broke down and he was received into care under Section 2 of the 1980 Child Care Act. At this time he was a well-built 16-year-old, six feet tall with a mass of dark hair and blue eyes.

At the point of disruption his adoptive mother wrote,

> The cause of all this emotional wear and tear [during 'disastrous' summer holidays] was, of course, Richard. I have with great sadness come to the

conclusion that I can no longer offer Richard a home . . . His one aim seems to be the disruption of this household. His monosyllabic responses . . . lead me to believe he derives some pleasure from my anguish. In return for food, TV, and money, his basic needs, he is willing to function at a minimal level. His deep seated resentment and hate towards me as a person is quite frightening. He has pursued a policy of silence at meal times and spent long hours alone in his room – a reflection of his inability to cope with the closeness of family life. I have tried to explain the consequences of his actions to Richard, and his only reply was 'I don't have to think'. I can only surmise that he does not wish to accept reality . . . I now feel we have reached the point of complete breakdown . . . I am not willing to have him home again.

This letter indicates the extraordinary stress faced by Richard and his adoptive family, even though, because of his attendance at boarding school, his time spent at home was minimal. It also illustrates Richard's main mechanism for coping with his pain – to cut himself off physically and emotionally from those around him.

Being concerned with such a stressful relationship cannot fail to have an effect on the social worker. Indeed, the worker's capacity to tolerate powerful and disturbing feelings is a recognised and important aspect of all work with children in trouble (this is explored in more detail in Chapters 1 and 8). Venetia comments, 'I have felt at times as confused and bewildered as Richard himself, suffering from feelings of hopelessness and despair and an inability to make sense of my work, let alone communicate the essential aspects of it in a coherent, balanced way.' The essential component of the work with Richard was to avoid becoming overwhelmed by the power of his feelings, through sustaining a capacity to tolerate his hopelessness, despair and sense of rejection.

Intervention with Richard

After making a full assessment of Richard's main problem areas, intervention could begin. There were two parts to Venetia Pigott's work. Firstly, she placed considerable emphasis on 'relationship' as a means of communicating and building up trust with Richard, so that they could begin to talk about the important, painful areas of his past. Given the difficulty Richard had in allowing anybody to get close to him, Venetia chose the use of 'shared experiences' (Winnicott 1977) to start her work. Secondly, she offered Richard the opportunity to construct a life story book, and actively engaged with him in this by taking him to revisit people and places from the past (see Ryan and Walker 1985).

Shared Experiences

Venetia writes:

> The extent of Richard's problems, and particularly, the difficulty that he had in relating to other people, put severe constraints on the way that it was possible to work with him. He was very suspicious of anybody in authority or in a parental role and his rapid retreat inside himself when he felt threatened made him extremely frustrating to be with, as the adoptive mother's letter indicates. Winnicott discusses the importance of 'a neutral zone of shared experience' in establishing communication with children and adolescents. She talks about these shared experiences – 'the ride in the car, or the game played together, or the TV programme watched, or even the visit to a clinic or hospital' (Winnicott 1977, p 45) – as an important part of the social worker's attempt to get alongside rather than be face-to-face with children. Richard and I had many 'shared experiences'. We travelled by car and by public transport, drank cups of coffee or ate meals together. Sometimes we talked and sometimes we were silent but, whatever we did, 'the shared experience' was an essential part of building our relationship.
>
> In common with many adolescents, Richard would often describe himself as feeling 'bored', this word being used to describe a wide variety of emotions which had little to do with boredom. After some months of work, his episodes of 'cutting-off' diminished, and only occurred when very painful subjects, such as his birth parents, the breakdown of his adoption or his relationship with his adoptive mother were mentioned. These topics often needed to be discussed during the process of statutory reviews, and his reactions were sometimes misinterpreted by those present as being a sign that Richard was 'not really interested' in the plans which were being made for him.

Visiting People and Places from the Past

Having established trust, Venetia suggested that they should begin a life story book. To help Richard piece together parts of his early life, it was agreed that Venetia should take him to revisit people from his past, and places where he used to live.

On a cold December day, after many conversations preparing Richard, I had arranged for us to go to London to meet Father Bell, an Anglican priest who had arranged Richard's adoption, and whom Richard had last seen when he was seven. We were later joined by Mrs Hopkins, the residential worker, who told Richard everything she could remember about his birth mother, the circumstances of his reception at the children's home and the details already mentioned. She gave him photographs of himself – kept for all these years. She made sense for him of some of his earliest memories. A lady in a green woolly hat who gave him chocolate and tonic water was his maternal grandmother. A chair which he remembered was one specially carved for him as a 'leaving present'. His mother was 'tall and looked like you, Richard, and she was so sad that she couldn't care for you any more'. Mrs Hopkins had met Richard's mother unexpectedly a few years after his adoption, she had asked how he was. She was clever and had obtained several O and A levels. We were all silent, intense while Mrs Hopkins spoke, moved by her warmth and understanding and the powerful emotions she evoked. I borrowed a camera, and Richard took photographs of us all and the outside of the children's home. Mrs Hopkins and Richard spent some time inside the home, building up more memories, more of Richard's identity. 'Am I a Roman Catholic?' Richard asked Father Bell. He explained that Richard was 'Church of England' and showed him the parish register, with details of his christening and godparents.

Venetia suggested to Richard that the information he had collected about his past should be made into a life story book. She had talked to him about doing a book with his foster mother and had given him a chronological list of the events in his life, feeling that they could be a resource for him, even if he did not use them as she had suggested. Venetia had deliberately decided that a life story book would be best done with his foster mother, who could be available over a longer period of time. It would also be an opportunity for them to develop their relationship. Richard chose not to follow up this idea, which both he and Venetia respected as being part of his need to make his own decisions.

Outcome

As time went on and Richard became easier to make contact with, he became more typically adolescent, taking an interest in his appearance and making more friends. His developing sense of identity and confidence was reflected in his attitude towards Venetia. He was able to express concern and consideration. He made better progress at school and seemed to have an easier relationship with his foster parents. He was even able to meet his adoptive mother again, and remarked 'It wasn't as bad as I thought it would be'. He said he now 'felt better' about her and, although he was unable to say why, he did say he felt 'safer' if Venetia was there. Venetia recognised the value of involving others indirectly in her intervention. Richard's foster family and teacher contributed to and collaborated with her own programme of direct work.

Venetia summarizes the outcome:

The scars remain. Emotionally Richard remains very much younger than his chronological age. There is a residue of suspicion and hostility. Intimacy, even with peers, is threatening and Richard will revert to stealing when he feels undervalued. However, there is little doubt that Richard has made considerable progress in his personal growth. I hope this will have provided him with a firmer foundation for dealing with some of the difficulties that lie ahead.

Sometimes, because children have not been as damaged as Richard, it is possible for them to recover enough from past losses to effect a completely successful transition from one family to another. This is well illustrated by Peter Daniel's work with Simon.

Simon

My overall aim was to help Simon, aged 6, resolve his uncertainty about whether his foster parents should become his adoptive parents. This could not be accomplished without the emotional participation of his foster parents. But before Simon could begin to make this transition, he needed to clarify and reinterpret past events. My relationship with him was the means by which he could feel secure enough to express his unresolved feelings about his birth family.

The issue for Simon was his experience of loss. He had shown some of his strong feelings about being separated and rejected by his mother, i.e. depression, denial, guilt and anger, but I was also aware of his overwhelming sense of feeling that somehow it was his fault. He would also frequently talk angrily of his mother's cohabitee whom he quite reasonably blamed for displacing him.

I had hoped during the course of our meetings to remove some of this sense of blame and badness from him and help him to understand more clearly his rejection in terms of his mother's own failings.

Prior to starting work with Simon, his behaviour indicated just how much he needed the kind of help envisaged. He had told his foster mother that he hated everyone, and asked questions such as 'Why was I taken from my grandmother?' (with whom he stayed briefly) or made statements such as 'My mum's boyfriend is keeping her locked away or else she would come and get me' and 'I don't want to be adopted because my mum will want to see me when she gets away from her boyfriend'. When I visited the same day he was angry and almost physically rigid. He withdrew and refused to speak. He was anxious and uncertain about his future. He suddenly became agitated, wanting to deal with his problems by 'shutting them out'. He was not ready to discuss his painful feelings of loss at this stage, but I hoped that as our relationship developed we could find more helpful ways of communicating some of this.

In planning the meetings it had been decided that the foster mother would be present during the sessions. It was recognized that she had an essential role to play, for, as the consistent carer, she was going to be left to 'pick up the pieces' regarding any emotional and behavioural problems that our discussions might induce. Furthermore, it was felt that her involvement would give her the opportunity to gain an understanding of Simon's needs, and a closeness to him. My relationship with the foster mother developed into an excellent working partnership.

We agreed on weekly meetings. It was important that Simon should be offered a regular schedule of contact for, as someone who had experienced so much rejection, the idea of continuity and consistency in my relationship with him was important. Also, to 'touch into' the painful areas of a child's experiences requires intensive work, and any gap or interlude would only have left him feeling abandoned, in the light of his past experiences.

I explained to Simon that I wanted to help him make sense of why he was in care, why he could not return home and why we hoped to place him for adoption.

The first couple of sessions were an attempt to build up trust. I wanted to go at Simon's pace and gain his trust through initial pleasurable experiences rather than painful ones, and I did not want him to associate me only with pain. I used trust games, e.g. drawing, and playing with clay, to allow him a sense of control through feeling and touching, and other games such as listing his 'likes' and 'dislikes'.

So far Simon had been very responsive and was beginning to gain in trust and confidence. At this stage, Simon's birth mother signed the initial 'Agreement to Adoption' form. The foster mother and I told Simon in a separate meeting and explained the difference between foster and adoptive care. I did not think he fully understood, but I felt it would become more evident as he learnt to interpret his various moves and separations.

Once we had gained Simon's trust we were ready to proceed to the next stage – by looking in detail at his various moves. We did not determine a fixed number of sessions. The duration of our work depended on the time it would take Simon to work through his problems.

We began by using a 'child ecomap', an idea borrowed from Vera Fahlberg. The aim was to help him understand what was happening to him in the 'here and now'. Some examples from the sessions are explained below.

We started by asking Simon, 'Why are you here?' He drew himself, and then replied. 'Because my mum prefers to live with her boyfriend.' He drew his first home in Hull and his foster home. He spoke about both with equal satisfaction – both represented security and happiness. He then drew his school and spoke fondly of various friends. Each session using the ecomap encouraged Simon's thoughts to come flooding out.

I asked Simon to draw his twin brothers (recently adopted). 'Do you remember why they were adopted?' I asked. 'My mum couldn't cope' were his exact words. He was not sure what this meant. I said she could not care for the twins and likewise she could not care for him. 'But she can cope with her boyfriend?' he asked. I tried to help him understand what 'coping' meant, and his mother's own problems. I explained how she was in poor health, that she needed a pacemaker, that she could not look after herself and that was why she needed her boyfriend to look after her. Simon seemed to be making sense of it.

We then chose a lighter subject, an exercise on 'dreams'. He said if his dreams could come true he wanted a motor bike, and to go around the world. The foster mother asked Simon what else he would like. He said he wanted to live in a family with three older children and two younger ones, with a mum and dad called Carol and Jock (the foster parents). There seemed no need for further explanation. Simon wrote this all on the 'ecomap'. The session had produced plenty of movement and Simon had shown that he was prepared to risk his feelings.

Further sessions covered other topics, including school and his brothers. The final stage had been planned to look in detail at Simon's moves. We had decided to use 'flow charts'. Very few young children have a clear concept of time and I felt that a flow chart specifying each move, with dates, would enable Simon to understand his past. Furthermore, it seemed likely that Simon would 'connect with' them more than with a more complex life-story book.

The plan was to give Simon his own book, where one page covered each move in his life. He was asked to draw from memory his own impression of each place he had lived. Dates were added, as well as a brief comment about each home (including foster homes) and the reasons why he had moved. Simon could not remember every place, or why he was sent there, and then I would give him an explanation to help him fill in the gaps in his understanding. The weekly sessions lasted for three months. We would usually spend one session at a time discussing a particular move in his life and the reasons behind it.

We agreed that our final session would be a visit to each address he had stayed at in his past, so that we could take a photograph to affix to each page. We added photographs of family and relatives. Simon's album was to be his own. It had helped him to unravel his confusion about his identity, and would be something he could refer to in the future. Each place and move was discussed in detail. As Simon began to learn about each move, his understanding of his mother's failure to care for him gradually became more evident.

Simon so enjoyed the sessions, which lasted for 3½ months, that exploring his background and finding his identity actually became fun for him. Even though we touched painful areas he was able to share his feelings freely, and the flow charts facilitated this.

His foster mother said she had noticed a real change in Simon. She described him as being a 'relaxed, happy boy who was enjoying life'. There were no longer problems at school. He was less withdrawn, and his aggressive outbursts were infrequent. He no longer wet the bed.

Simon made the following comments when summing up our meetings. These are presented verbatim:

> It settles my problems and troubles. I feel happier and fine. I don't get so angry. I would like to see my mum but it would be impossible because of Bill [her boyfriend]. My mum needs someone to look after her and so she can't look after anybody else. I just accept that is how she is. I don't feel angry or sad, but I do towards Bill. I would like to see my two little brothers!

Simon has still some way to go, to continue to talk through some of his feelings. In the meantime, the foster parents have applied to adopt Simon. I am sure some of his feelings are still smouldering and that he will need all the help he can get from his new parents. At least their involvement in the meetings has brought them closer to him and an understanding of his needs and feelings, and Simon is now ready for a new family.

It is now three years since Simon was adopted. He continues to make excellent progress and has become a well-established member of his permanent family.

The work with Patrick, Richard and Simon was difficult for the workers but, in each case, though progress was variable, there was a positive outcome for the child and his family. Several themes emerge as guidelines for direct work with emotionally damaged children.

1 The need for a positive approach in the worker – a belief that some change can occur.
2 The value of setting objectives that are realistic. A short programme of direct work can only begin to repair substantial emotional damage.
3 A capacity to be sensitive – not to force the pace of work but to persevere with children who are able to look at painful past experiences.
4 A recognition that the relationship with the worker and the process of work can be of considerable value to children, as well as any achieved outcome.
5 The need to remember and involve appropriately significant adults in the child's network.

5 Permanency Planning for Older Children in Care *Jane* Aldgate with *Janet Galley*

All children coming into care are faced with making new attachments to their carers, although the nature of these will vary according to the purpose of the placement, the needs of the child and the capacity of the carers. This chapter concentrates on children whose need is for a permanent alternative family.

It is difficult to estimate exactly the number of children in care who might need a new family. Most attempts to estimate numbers have been concerned with children who are adopted. Hapgood (1984) suggests that the number of children needing adoption might be around 6400, many of whom are of school age or older. Between 1974 and 1984 the proportion of all children adopted under ten dropped, whereas the proportion of children age ten or over increased by 60% (see *Adoption and Fostering*, Vol 10, No 3, 1986). Not all of these were children in care; the figures include children of single and divorced parents being adopted by parents and step-parents. For children in care, who cannot return to their families of origin, the policy emphasis has been increasingly on finding permanent placements. This trend is reflected in the growth of evaluative reports on various schemes (see, for example, Wedge and Thoburn 1986) but the tendency to equate permanency exclusively with adoption (DHSS 1984a) is unfortunate and could be misleading. Though statistics are difficult to find, some researchers and practitioners believe that, for older children in particular, this is only one option: long-term foster care or custodianship are equally viable alternatives for some (Triseliotis 1985).

The placing of older children in permanent alternative families is not without problems. Children come into care, and then into new families, bringing with them their own family and personal histories. There is a good deal of evidence to show that many of these young people are highly vulnerable, often having long-standing behavioural and emotional problems. In spite of this, the outcome looks extremely promising. Rushton and Treseder, for example, assert that 'there should be no doubt that where permanent substitute families can be found, these placements have a high probability of positive outcome', (Rushton and Treseder 1986, p 54). To support their view that older children are capable of developmental recovery, they draw on research evidence from five major studies, summarised in the following table:

Studies of Placement of Older Children

Author	Total research sample	No. of late placed children	Age at follow-up	Outcome
Kadushin (1970)	91 ex-foster care	N = 91 5 to 11 at placement	Adolescent interview with adopters only	Very high rate of satisfaction by adopters (85%) Problems were surmountable
Tizard and Hodges (1978)	30 adopted from institutions	N = 5 4.5 to 7.5 years at placements	Child assessed at 8 years and interview with parents	Close mutual attachments but some continuing behavioural and relationship problems
Lambert (1981) NCDS	37 ex-residential or foster care	N = 6 over 2 and under 7 at placements	7, 11 and 16 Tests and rating scales	Good progress but a suggestion that late placed children had poorer behaviour and reading scores
Triseliotis and Russell (1984)	44 adoptees ex-residential care	N = 14 between 4 and 8	Interviews with adoptees in mid-twenties	82% of total positive about the adoptive experience – satisfaction not related to age at placement
Thoburn et al (1985)	21 'Hard to place' children	N = 13 6 to 11 at placement	Developmental Assessment 2 years after placement	Placements continuing successfully, but only partial recovery for older children whose degree of attachment depended on the nature of their earlier experience

Source: *Adoption and Fostering*, Vol 10, No 3. (1986) p 55. Reproduced by kind permission of the authors and of the Editor, *Adoption and Fostering*.

Rushton and Treseder urge that care should be taken in generalizing from these findings:

> The children in each of the samples may have had quite different histories and types of adversity before their final placement, be displaying different levels of difficulty at the time of transfer and vary in their eagerness to move to a new home . . . However, the conclusion that investigators have mostly drawn from their studies is that many factors may influence the course and outcome of a placement but the best predictors of success are the attitudes, emotional climate and nature of the new parent–child relationships. (Rushton and Treseder 1986, pp 55–6)

If Rushton and Treseder are right, and attitudes, emotional climate and nature of new parent–child relationships are important predictors of success, then there would seem to be three major tasks for the social worker, which are necessary when preparing a placement. Firstly, there is the readiness of the families to receive children. Families need to be well motivated, flexible (Fitzgerald et al 1982b) and, above all, realistic about what they may expect from a child. From a consumer study of the views of long-term foster parents on disruption, Aldgate and Hawley (1986) found that families need adequate information and details of children's difficulties, with concrete examples of the context in which these problems may manifest themselves. Families should not be pressurized into taking children who will not 'fit' into their existing family patterns. They should be treated as colleagues rather than clients, with priority being given to the families' own views of what help they need in order to make a placement work. Requests for support and information should be taken at face value and dealt with in a straightforward and businesslike manner. Families need a high level of tolerance of stress (Thoburn 1985) and may also require tolerance of a child's dependent behaviour over time (Tizard 1977).

The second feature of successful outcome is children's readiness for placement (Fitzgerald 1983). Children need to have made sense of their past, which may involve some reworking of painful experiences (see Chapter 4). Older children must have been given 'psychological permission' by their former carers or parents to make new attachments. Children need to be well-motivated, and prepared to make the placement work (Fitzgerald et al 1982b). Children's wishes in this respect are very important, and, although it is clearly wrong to place the burden of decision-making on the shoulders of young children (Atherton 1986b), the older child, and, in particular the adolescent, has a right, both legally and morally, to a consideration of his or her wishes.

Furthermore, in arranging placement, 'children's views should be taken into account in the selection process, because they can understand their own needs and can communicate them if only adults will listen!' (Fitzgerald et al 1982b, p 23). Sadly, consumer research into children in care (Page and Clarke 1977 and Stein and Ellis 1983) demonstrates that children's views are often not taken directly into account in making decisions about their lives. Not listening to children's opinions about what they feel and what they want may jeopardize a placement (Triseliotis 1985). Take, for example, the young person who did not want to move from his children's home to a distant foster home because he wished to retain contact with his mother who was in hospital. He also made it clear that his mother represented the only family that he wanted. In spite of this, and because the children's home was closing, he was moved to a foster home where, before long, there was a traumatic disruption, with the boy assaulting the daughter of the foster family. The family themselves attributed the disruption to the boy's anger and resentment about plans to which he had neither overtly or covertly agreed (Aldgate and Hawley 1986).

Thirdly, plans for a placement should take into account the individual requirements of the child, and the ways in which they mesh with those of the new family. As Maluccio et al suggest (1986), there can be many variations of permanence, provided the basic parameters of stability and continuity of relationships to promote children's growth and functioning are met. To this end, Thoburn catalogues 16 routes for permanence for children who cannot be rehabilitated with their own families. They are as follows:

1 Secure fostering with the current foster family;
2 Secure fostering with a new foster family;
3 Custodianship with foster parents or relatives with whom the child is already living;
4 Placement before custodianship with known relatives or friends;
5 Foster placement with strangers with a view to custodianship if all goes well;
6 Foster placement with a new family with a view to adoption if all goes well;
7 Foster placement leading quickly to adoption;
8 Placement directly for adoption.
The eight routes can each be with or without contact with natural parents or siblings placed elsewhere, making 16 routes in all. (Thoburn 1985, p 30)

These routes depart from the idea that permanence involving new attachments can only be achieved through adoption. Triseliotis (1985) and Thoburn (1985) make it abundantly clear that adoption is not necessarily appropriate for many older children in care. It will nonetheless remain one important option and, for some children and families, its legal framework will be a necessary part of providing an overall sense of security. Others may more appropriately use custodianship, or welcome the continuing support from social workers which can be part of permanent foster care. It is certainly not fair to mislead children into expecting adoption, if this is unrealistic and unobtainable (Thoburn 1985). One major problem is that the current legal system is not well suited to the pursuit of these different options (Ormrod 1983). Adoption conveys a sense of finality; custodianship may be revoked; and foster care, even where the local authority holds parental rights, can offer no legal certainty about the future. But does this matter? In the end, what may be the determining factors of success are the commitment and attitudes of all concerned. This issue is well demonstrated in the following work by Janet Galley.

Background

Joyce is the illegitimate daughter of Dianne. She was brought up by her maternal grandmother in Manchester until the age of six. Her mother was working abroad, and took no responsibility for her upbringing. When she was six, 'Gran' had to go into hospital, and Dianne's sister and brother-in-law, Lynn and Tony, who live in the Home Counties, went up to Manchester to get Joyce. They were appalled by the conditions she was living in. The house was dirty and Joyce's bedclothes were soaked in urine. They resolved that she should not return to Manchester. They requested help from their local Social Services Department and Joyce was received into care, Section 2 1980 Act (S.1 1948 Act). Parental Rights were assumed four months later on the grounds that Dianne had 'persistently failed to discharge the obligations of a parent'. Joyce has remained with Lynn and Tony ever since.

Family Structure

Foster family

Tony Hammond	aged 46	Lorry driver
Lynn Hammond	aged 42	Housewife/Seamstress

Children

Kevin Hammond	aged 21	Caterer, British Rail
Karen Hammond	aged 20	Shop assistant
Neil Hammond	aged 19	Paint sprayer, car bodies
Joyce Curtis	aged 17	Car valet
Chris Hammond	aged 14	At school

Natural Family

Emily Curtis (known as Davies)	aged 70	Maternal grandmother in Manchester
Mr Davies (deceased)		Common law husband
Lynn Hammond		(Joyce's foster mother) brought up by her maternal grandparents (Joyce's great-grandparents)
Dianne Theodorakis	aged 34	(Joyce's mother) married and living in Greece
Peter Curtis	aged 38	Maternal uncle, Caterer, Lake District
Chris Curtis	aged 46	Maternal uncle, in Manchester

I have known Joyce and her foster family for five years. The description they gave me of the little girl they collected from Manchester was of a frightened, dirty, smelly and disturbed child. She was said to lie, steal and be a persistent bed-wetter. She had burn marks on her knuckles, which she said 'Gran' had done on the fire grate as a punishment for stealing. She had remained somewhat sullen and uncommunicative over the years, and still wet the bed occasionally. The foster family had experienced some difficult times with her, but, on the whole, they were fond of her and regarded her as an accepted and permanent member of her family. Apart from one telephone call some years previously they had had no contact from Joyce's mother, Dianne, and no contact from maternal grandmother Mrs Davies.

I met the family after the case had remained unallocated for about nine months as it was seen as a non-urgent 'relative foster home' placement. Joyce was notorious for not speaking to social workers and I set about establishing a relationship with her.

By this time she had begun using the surname of her foster family and they asked about the possibility of its being legally changed through adoption. We agreed that we should begin to explore this and I arranged to talk to Joyce about her wishes, using life story work. As a result of this work we decided together not to take any futher action in relation to the adoption.

Joyce again expressed an interest in adoption when Dianne, her birth mother, appeared on the scene 2 years later. She had been married to a Greek national but was now divorced and living in London. I met her and she paid several visits to Joyce. The foster family received her well, she acted responsibly towards Joyce and agreed we should pursue adoption if Joyce wished. Then she disappeared again and reappeared the next year, telling us all she had remarried and was back in Greece.

Throughout that year, Joyce and her mother corresponded; in the summer of the next year, Dianne came to this country for her brother Peter's wedding. Joyce's attendance at the wedding re-united her with several family members whom she had not met for many years.

Once Joyce had reestablished contact with her mother, we agreed we would not pursue a decision about adoption until she and Dianne had given each other a chance to become better acquainted. It was at this point that I started working more intensively with Joyce.

Joyce is a tall, well-built girl with short, brown hair and angular features. She has a broad, attractive smile, but, when not smiling, she can still look sullen. She finds it hard to express herself verbally. She left school at 16, having obtained CSEs, and had just started a Youth Training Scheme in office work. I saw her approximately once a month over several months, usually on her own, but occasionally with members of her family. The focus of my work was to try to help Joyce work on her identity and make a decision about adoption. At the same time, I was conducting parallel work with the foster family and, sporadically, with Joyce's own mother.

Following the family wedding that summer, Dianne told Joyce she did not wish her to be adopted. Joyce was upset after Dianne had got drunk at the wedding and had not written to her since. Nevertheless, she confirmed that she did not now wish to be adopted, but would like to change her name by Deed Poll (something a neighbour had a neighbour had suggested). I took this to be a sign of her ambivalent feelings towards her foster family and her mother and suggested to Joyce that we spend some time discussing this. (My own feelings were that she clearly 'belonged' in her foster family and adoption was the obvious way of confirming this.)

We drew a family tree, showing clearly all the family surnames. Her own legal surname clearly did not confer any real sense of belonging because so few family members used it – to her knowledge only Uncle Peter and Uncle Chris (whom she didn't know very well). When asked to put herself in the tree, she placed herself firmly in her foster family.

I used Fahlberg's three parent circles (see Fahlberg 1981b, p 19) to look at Joyce's position in relation to the Social Services Department, her birth mother and her foster parents. These circles divide parenting into three parts – birth parents, legal parents and 'parenting' parents. For foster children, the roles are split. Joyce quickly picked up the point of the exercise, identifying appropriate tasks for each 'parent' and without hesitation identifying her foster parents as her 'caring parents'.

I then used the same circles to show her the difference between Deed Poll and Adoption. I explained to her that the final decision was hers, and that after Christmas we would meet for her to tell me what she had decided. Over this time, she only had sporadic contact by letter with her mother and no further discussion about the proposed adoption with her.

After Christmas, Joyce became quite unsettled. She wanted to leave home and get a job as a nanny; she stopped going to college for her office training. She ordered, then cancelled, and then re-ordered, new clothes. She was still unable to tell me what she had decided to do about her name, and I felt she was acting out her confusion.

I thought about my role and decided I was probably adding to her confusion in two ways. Firstly, because I had already committed myself to the idea of adoption, I could not really take on board the idea of Deed Poll. I thought Joyce was picking up my feelings about this. I also felt that I had become rather too focussed on Joyce's status when there were clearly so many issues about her identity, and where she belonged, that she was uncertain and frightened about. In order to help Joyce regain some sense of control and security, and to help her focus more on the feelings that had been stirred up by this issue, I acted more assertively. I refused permission for her to leave home (which she accepted without a fight) and told her she must either go back to college or get another job. I also agreed to put the necessary arrangements for a Deed Poll into effect. This activity on my part eased the situation considerably. Relationships at home improved and Joyce did get herself another job, as a car valet, which she enjoys.

In February Joyce received an invitation to visit Dianne in Greece. This seemed a good opportunity for her to talk to her birth mother about the Deed Poll. I discussed this with Joyce and wrote to Dianne. The holiday was fixed for April; between February and April, I confirmed all necessary arrangements for a Deed Poll. All parties at this stage agreed we should go ahead.

Joyce became the centre of considerable attention for the very best of reasons, with the whole family caught up in the excitement of the trip. None of them had been abroad, or in an aeroplane. She had extra money spent on her and became visibly more assured. By the time the holiday arrived, Joyce had been happily settled in her job for four months. Disagreements with her foster family had diminished considerably. She had new clothes, a new hair-do and was looking more lively and bright than I had seen her for a long time. She was quite clear about the Deed Poll and felt no qualms about discussing it with Dianne.

The position as I write is that Joyce has just returned from Greece after a very successful holiday. She was the centre of attention, with her own bedroom and lots of money spent on her, and had been given many treats. Although Dianne signed the agreement for the Deed Poll and said she would agree to whatever Joyce wished, Joyce has now decided she will not change her name after all. Having the two names isn't really all that much of a problem, as she's managed for eighteen years and she's going back to Greece for three months next year!

I'm sure there will be other developments as she moves towards her 18th birthday but I feel Joyce has managed to establish a place for herself with her mother and her foster family which both she and they feel comfortable with. As this has become clearer, the issue of her name has become less significant; she dismissed it as of no importance on my last visit. She was saying, 'I am who I am, I'm comfortable with this; the name in itself is no longer necessary in order for me to confirm this'.

Janet's case study demonstrates several factors involved in helping children to make new attachments. Firstly, children and their families need to find the plan for the future which best suits them. A blanket approach to permanency is not helpful, as Janet found. Her own assumption was that adoption was the only way to confirm the relationships which already existed. However, once she could free herself from her own priorities and prejudices and allow Joyce and her family to find their own way to a solution, a resolution of the issues emerged. Janet learnt from her work 'to be aware of my own motives and wishes and their influence on how cases develop. I am sure my reluctance about a Deed Poll conveyed itself to Joyce and added to her confusion. It did not give her more space in the way I hoped'.

Secondly, Janet's work demonstrates how a young person's sense of identity is a factor to be taken into account when that person is establishing himself or herself in a family. This concept is explained in Chapter 6 in some depth, with particular reference to work with ethnic minority children, but is considered briefly here. Triseliotis believes that there are three areas which may make a large contribution to identity building:

1. A childhood experience of feeling wanted and loved within a secure environment.
2. Knowledge about one's background and personal history.
3. The experience of being perceived by others as a worthwhile person.
(Triseliotis 1983, p 23)

Janet helped Joyce build her identity in several stages. At an early point in her work she did a life story book which clarified many of the events in Joyce's early life. Then with the help of a family tree and Fahlberg's circles, she helped Joyce reconcile the different, but compatible, elements of her psychological and biological parenting. This allowed Joyce to complete her sense of 'social identity' (Haimes and Timms 1985).

Joyce's situation is by no means unique. Many older children in care may desire a new family who can offer them 'inclusive permanence' (Aldgate 1984), allowing them to fulfil their need to retain links with their birth families. Triseliotis believes that this is perfectly acceptable: 'Children can develop their personality and identity within the concept of two sets of parents, provided there is clarity in their minds about what is happening and that the stability and continuity of care is maintained and not threatened.' (Triseliotis 1983, p 31.) He supports his case by citing the growing body of evidence from divorce studies which suggests that the maintenance of contact with non-custodial parents is important to children's emotional development (see Triseliotis 1983). The critical factor for success may lie in the adults concerned not seeing themselves as rivals for children's affections, but offering something different and complementary (Jenkins 1981, Benians 1982, Adcock 1984).

Social workers can have a clear role to play in helping the different parties reach a resolution. Birth parents may often feel that 'the price of the permanent plan is admission of parental failure' (Jackson and Dunne 1981, p 154). These parents will need help in their own right to free them from their former responsibilities (Boswell 1981) yet enhance their sense of competence by recognizing their continuing, valuable role as information-givers. Janet Galley achieved this transition with Joyce's mother Dianne. She writes:

> I have been able to clarify with Dianne the roles and responsibilities of the various parties and so far she has not tried to usurp the foster parents' role as Joyce's psychological parents. At the same time, we have been able to establish an equally important role for her in providing links with the past for Joyce (in particular, information about Joyce's natural father) and enhancing Joyce's self-image by being reliable and consistent in her contact. She has, on the whole, fulfilled this, and appears to have formed the basis of a mutually satisfying relationship with Joyce.

Janet Galley's work with Dianne would have had little effect on Joyce without parallel work being conducted simultaneously with Lynn and Tony. One of the main things she achieved was helping them to feel secure enough in their own relationship with Joyce to allow her to make contact and build a new relationship with Dianne. Janet writes:

> Lynn and Tony were very reluctant at first to encourage visits from Dianne. They regarded her as unreliable and a bad influence. They were already experiencing problems with Joyce's adolescent behaviour and felt visits from Dianne would make this worse. However, at the same time, Lynn felt it might help to improve relationships within the wider family if they resumed contact.
>
> I felt their reluctance was in part due to their own uncertainties about their relationship with Joyce, which seemed to be reflected in the way they were handling her adolescence. I felt if I could help

them, particularly Lynn, feel more confident about their relationship with Joyce they would be confident about contact with Dianne. So I concentrated on helping Lynn and Tony identify the strengths and the importance of their relationship with Joyce. With Joyce's permission, I shared with them her view of them as 'caring parents'. With their permission, I shared with Joyce their anxieties about contact with Dianne. This enabled Joyce to express some of her anxieties about being made to leave her foster home against her wishes. We aired all this at a family meeting at which Lynn and Tony were able to say to Joyce that they cared very much about her, that they wanted what was best for her and whatever she decided to do would not change their feelings for her. Joyce was able to tell them she wanted to stay with them and would like to get to know Dianne better without jeopardizing this.

Establishing contact with Dianne opened the way to reestablishing contact with Lynn and Joyce's wider family, particularly 'Gran', whom none of them had seen for years. This proved a gold mine of information for both Lynn and Joyce. It is also important to note that Joyce's problems related not only to the relationship with her biological mother and her sense of identity as a child in care, but also to general problems of identity in adolescence.

Janet concludes:

The outcome, at the time of writing, has been successful. By having the confidence to 'let go' and let Joyce establish her identity in her own way, Lynn and Tony have been able to keep her and her affections. They have been rewarded by seeing Joyce return from Greece yet again (despite niggling doubts that she wouldn't!) smiling, happy, pleased to see them and laden with presents. They have said directly to Joyce that whatever she decides about adoption makes no difference to their feelings for her and have demonstrated it by their actions. This has, in turn, allowed Joyce to find her own way to a resolution of her problems. All this has been achieved without any serious breakdown of relationships and with links with the wider family strengthened, a remarkable and impressive achievement for them all, which I have said to them.

Throughout her work with Joyce and her two families, Janet had to make some adjustments to her own attitudes about what constitutes a permanent alternative family. In our multi-cultural society, family diversity is the 'norm' (See Rapoport, Fogarty and Rapoport 1982). With a high divorce rate, polynuclear families are becoming more commonplace, with children relating to parents and step-parents and a wide range of kin. A greater acceptance of diversity, and observation of how children may relate successfully to parents who are living apart, may reassure us about the value of maintaining links between children in permanent alternative families and their birth families. In this respect, Atherton (1986a) believes that much can be learnt about part-time parenting from studying the family patterns of some Afro-Caribbean families. Millham et al (1986) urge us to account for another factor:

> Links have a power dimension. Actual contact may not be necessary when the participants have power to intervene and change the situation should the need arise. In our earlier work in preparatory schools, for example, we were often surprised by children's statements that they felt close to their parents in situations when they saw them infrequently, perhaps when parents were overseas. It was clear that perceptions of links did not correspond with the frequency of contact and children felt close to absent parents who they knew would act in their interest as and when necessary. (Millham et al 1986, p 16)

Developments in theory and practice over the past few years have improved the prospects of older children finding new families. We can be optimistic about the capacity of many children to recover reasonably well from early adversity. Practice has reached a point of sophistication where family-finding may include a wide range of placements, which can be adopted to meet the needs of individual children. Further success will depend upon continuing recruitment of families who can provide diversity and who, for older children, are prepared to offer 'inclusive permanence' as a major option.

6 White Social Workers/Black Children: Issues of Identity

Nadine Brummer

A decade or more ago there were only a handful of texts for social workers addressing questions of cross-cultural social work. Today their titles and some of their content seem condescending and, indeed, racist, as perhaps the current concepts, practice and thinking of white social work educators and practitioners will seem a decade on from now.

The very title, *Social Work with Coloured Immigrants and their Families* (Triseliotis 1972), for example, now seems disconcerting not only because language has changed or is changing but also because some of the content aimed at white workers could now be perceived as out of place. Kent (1972), for instance, in a discussion of value differences between white caseworkers and immigrant clients, advises white social workers to think analogously of work with delinquents, mentally ill people or 'Eastenders' of working-class origin.

Similarly, two decades ago, black children needing substitute family care, for whatever reasons, were thought of as 'hard to place children' and bracketed with physically or mentally handicapped children.

Although there have been shifts in conceptualizing the social work task in a society that is nominally multi-racial or multi-cultural, social work practitioners are still grappling with feelings of inadequacy, in both a theoretical and a practical sense. This is especially so in inner city conurbations where the bulk of the workload might well consist of work with black families and children; it is even more so in areas where there is no apparent significant black presence. It is precisely because our society at present is in many senses only nominally multi-racial that it is difficult to get a firm purchase on the key issues. Not only are we unsure of how different ethnic groups relate to each other, but we are also unsure of how individuals of different origins relate to or communicate with each other. More specifically, there is uncertainty about how both black and white professionals communicate with each other and with their clients.

Considerable evidence now exists of the objective experience of people of Afro–Caribbean and Asian origin, and their lack of access to housing, jobs, education and the life chances which these bring (Smith 1977, Brown 1984). Although there is no ideology of racism in the United Kingdom, i.e. no overt statements or policies which ascribe inferior status to black people, there is considerable evidence to suggest that racism is an endemic part of British society (see, for example, Dummett 1973, Husband 1986). Institutionalized racism, the combination of prejudice and power which ensures that black minorities are oppressed by the white majority, is a fact of our major social institutions, and structures the life experiences of most black people.

I have chosen the concept of identity as one which may usefully serve to integrate the many and diverse themes inherent in this subject, in a society where negative stereotypes of black people, and consequent racial abuse, can lead to strongly negative feelings about personal worth. In a society in which negative stereotypes abound, children of Asian and Afro–Caribbean origin are especially vulnerable to these feelings. Negative comments made, albeit thoughtlessly, about their food, their language or characteristic speech inflections and pronunciations, clothes or religious beliefs and traditions can lead to a feeling that the life-styles of their families should be hidden rather than acknowledged. A sense of shame overlays an appropriate sense of pride in, and enjoyment of, their cultural heritage. While it is not possible to address all the issues connected with the needs of black children in care, and while not intending to offer prescriptions for practice, this chapter will explore the key concerns. These are complex and interrelated.

The key issues are:

1 The concept of identity.
2 Research into the self-concept of black children.
3 Black children in care – issues of assessment.
4 Resources for black children: the debate about same-race placement.
5 Direct work with black children.

The Concept of Identity

Identity is both a familiar and an imprecise notion, to which we give more thought when there is dislocation or loss. Typically most of us ask, 'Who or what am I?' at the life crises of adolescence and the mid-years. For some people, however, self-questioning is a norm, and self-confidence something only achieved through struggle.

There are several theoretical perspectives from which the concept of identity is viewed – ego psychology (Erikson 1968, 1969), social psychology (Tajfel 1974) and social learning theory (Ausubel 1984 and Maximé 1986) to name but a few. 'Self-sameness' through time, self-image/self-concept, self-esteem, a sense of belonging to a distinctive group which might have a racial and/or ethnic dimension – all of these are subsumed under the umbrella term 'identity'.

Erikson's formulations (1968, 1969) are helpful in furthering our understanding of identity. He describes three aspects:

Ego identity

The 'I' which persists through changes of time and place and changes in personal, bodily characteristics, as in ageing or handicapping conditions, etc. This 'I' brings together an awareness of time past, dreams and present perceptions – in Erikson's words, the 'synthesizing ego'.

Personal identity

A recognition that despite changes, a central core of sameness exists recognizably for self and others with whom one has related over time. Certainly when one meets an older relative who exclaims, 'You haven't changed a bit!' one might feel insulted or flattered, but also reassured.

Group identity

A sense of being connected with a specific cultural group which has characteristic ways of organizing and transmitting experiences. There may well be a difference between self-definition (e.g. 'I come from a Catholic German family') and description by others ('a typical white'). This concept of group identity has obvious affinity with ethnic identity.

However, racial identity is more closely connected with colour. Small states, 'If a healthy personality is to be formed, the psychic image of the child must merge with the reality of what the child actually is. That is to say, if the child is black (reality), he or she must first recognize and accept that he or she has a black psychic image' (Small 1986, p 88).

White workers need to address their own ethnicity; they are members of different groups, differentiated by religion, social class and provenance, to which there may be long-standing allegiances, accompanied by unexamined identifications. Mostyn, for example, refers to

Freud's use of the term 'ethnic identity' when he tried to formulate his link with the Jewish people. Freud talked of an 'inner identity' which links individuals with the unique values and history of their people – 'the safe privacy of a common mental construction' (Mostyn 1972, p 98). This comment supports the notion of giving individuals 'permission' to feel identified with others, even if those others are physically and geographically separated. Ethnic identity becomes a kind of anchorage, more so because there is a fusion between the inner sense of self and the external feeling of solidarity.

In thinking about identity definitions, several points need to be made. Firstly, current theories of personality development lack a developmental perspective for black children and young people (Logan 1981). Secondly, white social workers' assessments of black children and their families are based on mono-cultural assumptions and white norms. What has not been taken into consideration is the fact that black children are subject to two sources of self-conceptualization – that from within the black community and that from without. A serious problem arises when there is a lack of congruence, and it is here that the risk of an identity crisis is high. The continuum of potential confusion might range from occasional doubts about acceptability at the mildest level, through to a total sense of disintegration in situations of extreme stress. Thirdly, as well as concerning themselves with the question of a child's sense of identity, it is important that workers come to an understanding of their own ethnic and racial origins and values. In preparing for social work intervention, workers need to confront their own feelings about living in a multi-cultural society and their feelings about cross-cultural encounters. White workers need to realise that 'ethnicity' is not just something that belongs to minorities.

Research into the Self-Concept of Black Children

Research into identity and self-concept is difficult to evaluate, and from there to extrapolate its meaning for practice. Studies have often not differentiated variables of age, sex, social class, along with the world views of different ethnic groups, which may or may not be compatible with 'mainstream' societies. Inconsistencies are perhaps due to a lack of clarity about precisely what is being researched, i.e. is it self-concept/-image, self-esteem, racial identity or ethnic identity, or social status? For a detailed, critical view of relevant studies see Foster-Carter (1986).

In spite of the difficulties of evaluation, studies carried out in the

1940s (Clark and Clark, 1974), seemed to have a consistent theme. Young black children identified themselves as white, whereas white children preferred to be who they were. For example, in response to questions about black and white dolls, when asked to say which doll was most like them, white children rarely picked out black dolls whereas black children often picked out white dolls. Furthermore black children seemed to prefer white children as friends and playmates, whereas white children tended to prefer white children.

The work of Clark and Clark has been replicated in Britain by Milner (1975). He concluded that, rather than children mis-identifying their racial origins, they tended to deny them. Additionally, Davey et al (1980) found that children who did not reject their own ethnic identity had good self-esteem or self-worth, but did perceive themselves as having lower social status. These findings lead to speculation that the importance of the research may lie in the questions posed rather than the answers. What are the experiences of black children that lead them to identify 'white with right', and to deny or reject their own racial or ethnic group?

Often, white workers and carers have difficulty in relation to the experiences of black children, and thereby add to their confusion. For example, a black four year old boy found to be scratching at his skin said to his white foster mother, 'I want to be white like you'. The reply, 'But we lie in the sun to be brown like you', demonstrates just how difficult it is to deal with these questions when carers themselves have not worked through the issues. A more appropriate response might be to explore the child's feelings which lie behind the question.

Cooper (1973) gives a case example of a five year old black child, Bernard, seen at a child guidance clinic because of temper outbursts and bedwetting. Bernard's parents had separated. His black paternal grandmother had spoken negatively about the unreliability of black men, their violence, and hyper-sexuality. Bernard, in the course of play therapy, sorted out black and white dolls into distinct piles; he made repeated slips of the tongue, interchanging 'white' and 'right' in describing the dolls. The white worker commented on his confusion and when Bernard repeated, 'white-right boys are nice', she launched into a race relations lecture, giving the didactic view of differences being not better or worse. What had been skilful work started to degenerate into premature reassurances, which made it difficult for Bernard to continue exploring his own feelings about race. He was told, rather than allowed, to discover important facts about differences, identity and self-esteem.

79

Black Children in Care – Issues of Assessment

Despite the absence of precise, analyzed national statistics it is generally agreed that there is a disproportionate number of black children in care (Arnold 1982, Cheetham 1986). Concern has been expressed about this for some time (Fitzherbert 1967; Rowe and Lambert 1973). The reasons for the phenomenon are complex; the social, economic and psychological effects of racial discrimination on black families are manifold, and the interactive process between black families and representatives of white social welfare institutions has yet to be documented adequately.

The way black families are conceptualized and assessed must have some bearing on why white social workers have seen so many black children as in need of care and protection. Fitzherbert (1967) pointed out the discrepancy between client and worker perspectives in the Fifties and early Sixties, at the time of immigration from the West Indies. While West Indian parents saw their problems as socio-economic, the result of bad housing and unemployment, white social workers saw black parents as deficient in parenting skills and capacities. Discrepancies in attitudes, and in definitions of problems, have not been confined to ethnic minority groups (see for example Packman 1986 and Fisher et al 1986) but the issue of race has often amplified the findings of other studies.

The way that black families have coped with the problems of survival in an alien and discriminatory culture has not been perceived as a strength, because workers have assessed black families on the basis of criteria applicable to white families. Sociological research is now beginning to explore black family patterns from a black rather than a traditional white perspective. A quotation from an American text could be equally applicable in Britain:

> Female dominated households were considered almost universal among poor blacks even when statistics showed they were not . . . The view that amongst blacks the nuclear family unit is disorganized or 'broken' because households do not contain a 'complete family', reflects the confusion of many on this issue. (Leigh and Green 1982, p 110)

The negative, pathologizing view of black families affected place-ment arrangements for children in care for many years, confining them to residential care. Alternative black carers were not sought and white families seemed unable to accept black children. In the early Seventies the stereotype of deficient black families was reinforced by the recognition of the difficulties faced by seven to fourteen year olds coming to the UK to rejoin parents who had often remarried. Children had to sever attachments from beloved grandparents, the loss sometimes leading to conflict in their new home and uncontainable behaviour, which in turn brought many of them into care. These multiple threats to identity – loss of homeland and stable carers, and loss of idealized image – were compounded by the loss of self-esteem which ensued. These children found themselves unable to 'fit into' a white-dominated society which failed to meet not just their emotional but even their physical needs, such as special skin care.

There are three crucial issues involved in the assessment of black children coming into care. Firstly, it is important for social workers to recognise family diversity, and develop a knowledge of black family functioning (Leigh and Green 1982). Secondly, concern about the disproportionate number of black children in care, however appropriate, must not deflect from a proper focus on child protection. Social workers' fears of being perceived as racist can lead to them applying a 'rule of optimism', to losing balanced judgement and fudging hard decisions (Blom-Cooper 1985). Thirdly, any intervention has to include not only an assessment of needs and risks, but also the development of resources more conducive to positive self-identity.

Resources for Black Children: the Debate about Same-Race Placement

It has only recently been acknowledged that the major resource for black children in need of substitute family care is likely to be other black, rather than white, carers. Concern over black children 'drifting' in care was translated in the Sixties into the active recruitment of white foster/adoptive parents – the so-called one-way traffic of black children. Small (1984, 1986) has written of the diverse motivations of transracial adopters. New insights came in the Seventies, from black professionals, about the implications of this for the black community, the donor-group who might lose their best resource, i.e. their children, and for the children who have to negotiate dispossession from their racial and kinship groups. Given that this is so, there must be professional and political concern that black children in predominantly white environments may be weakened in their capacity to cope with the hostility that may come their way, when the outside world relates to them more as a social category than as the individuals which they would be in their families.

Gill and Jackson's book, *Adoption and Race* (1983), a follow-up study of 36 families with transracially placed children, focussed attention once again on the criteria used in assessing the outcome of transracial placements. Against conventional criteria of success, e.g. adjustment in family group, and social and academic competence at school, these children were doing very well but most regarded themselves as 'brown' or 'coloured' and did not feel any identification with the black community. These findings caused grave concern among many professionals, spearheaded by the National Association of Black Social Workers in England.

Transracial placements have caused equal concern in the USA. Jenkins (1982) found that while black professionals were committed to same-race placements, black parents' primary concern was for a 'loving home'. This discrepancy was accounted for by Jenkins as a result of the wishes of black parents for their children 'to make out in white society'. She argues that it is in the arena of 'mixing or matching' that commitment to ethnic-sensitive practice is best demonstrated.

Despite the many professional and political arguments for same-race placements (Gill and Jackson 1983, Cheetham 1982), the issue remains contentious (Cheetham 1986). There is a risk that white social workers may pay lip service to policies of matching where such policies have been introduced, rather than give their full commitment to the implementation of these policies. The perceived immediacy of the attachment needs of young children is often seen to be in conflict with the extensive recruitment required for 'suitable families'.

Recruitment methodology needs, and in some places is getting, attention. Myths and stereotypes of suitability for parenting need challenging; diversification of parenting does not mean the lowering of standards in child care. Planning for permanency must mean the application of a range of options which takes account of the significance of racial origin and the reality of a racist society.

Particular problems arise for children of mixed parentage. A commonly expressed concern of white practitioners is the fear of imposing a black identity on children of mixed parentage who actively refuse placement in a black home. This is typically a dilemma for adolescents. Collusion with white mothers separated from black partners who encourage their children to lie ('Tell them you're of Mediterranean origin') is not uncommon. It is important for social workers not to collude with these explanations. The bitterness of the spoiled or broken relationship should not find a convenient focus in colour, denying the presence of other factors. Children of mixed parentage need both a sense of belonging and the capacity to negotiate differences. The principle which should underpin good practice is that identity issues require exploration rather than denial.

Direct Work with Black Children

Many social workers, both black and white, are working with great sensitivity and dedication with black children. White social workers have to face several questions, of which three are discussed here. Firstly, there is the question of assessment, and the adequacy of the theoretical basis for work; secondly, work with adult attachment figures; and thirdly, the importance of exploring what the child is really thinking and feeling. I take for granted the fact that play as well as speech is a way for children to communicate and that play-materials for black children must include the kind of dolls, paints, masks, books which enable both child and worker to reflect on sameness and difference of colour. An example of the consequences of not taking these factors into account is shown in the case of Dawn.

Dawn

Dawn, a ten-year-old of Afro-Caribbean origin, had a history of multiple moves between parents, friends, relatives, foster parents and institutions. All had managed only short periods of care over the past eight years, because of Dawn's behavioural problems. One plan to rehabilitate her with her father and his new co-habitee had recently failed because neither could tolerate her stealing and lying. Dawn herself expressed a longing to return to her adored aunt, who was adamant that she could not offer her a permanent home. Dawn's problem, therefore, was that she needed a home with people who could tolerate her behavioural difficulties.

The worker's initial assessment of Dawn was based on attachment theory within the context of a white nuclear family. Dawn's behavioural, emotional and cognitive development to date was explained in terms of her lack of continuous and dependable relationships. But attachment theory, in the Eurocentric sense of child-rearing within the nuclear family, is not necessarily enough to help workers understand and plan for children from diverse family backgrounds. The worker would need to have assessed Dawn's moves within the context of her family network, asking whether the family, though dispersed, was nonetheless a responsible group with obligations mutually shared between different members, or whether the moves were precipitate, rejecting, hostile and therefore unacceptable to black community norms. In this sense, could the worker herself explore the reality of the family's kinship system without either idealizing the extended family as 'able and willing to look after its own', or rejecting alternative patterns of family care? This issue raises once again the necessity of social workers having a sound knowledge of family diversity, and adequate supervision. Social workers also need to beware of explaining problems by reference to ethnocentric theories of individual and family functioning.

Secondly, as an aware practitioner, the worker realised there was a paradox in her offering herself in direct work as an attachment figure with whom trust could develop, to be transferred subsequently to a permanent carer. The paradox is as follows: she did not want this black child to identify black abandoning parents as 'bad' and white carers as 'good', but somehow felt at a loss in coping with the strong developing attachment to herself. The child clearly wanted to see her as the good mother and asked her for West Indian food. Although 'tuning in' to Dawn's many needs, and helping her rebuild and regain a sense of control, the worker was nonetheless unable to explore with Dawn what she was really thinking and feeling about her blackness and the worker's whiteness, even when the child was offering cues for such an exploration.

In this example, Dawn can be seen trying to integrate black values with those of white workers; she asks the worker for West Indian food and asks her about her aunt's country, as if maintaining a hope that somehow her heritage could be valued by the white worker and transmitted to her. The worker felt she could not authentically transmit what was not her own, and, more significantly, could not address the issues even when they arose in a very direct form.

Prescription is easy; practice is hard. One point being made here is that in cross-cultural work with children, white workers need to maintain the balance between addressing the subjective experiences of the child, without forcing the issue of ethnicity, and acknowledging the importance of addressing, rather than politely ignoring, issues of ethnicity and colour when they emerge in the work as *central* to the experience of the child.

Some Points for Further Deliberation

This introduction to some of the practical and theoretical issues confronting white social workers dealing with black children has necessarily been both selective and condensed. The central argument of the chapter has been that, in a society which is institutionally racist, any devaluing of black people needs to be countered by an appraisal of what goes into the personal, social and ethnic construction of a positive identity for black children in care. Ahmed et al (1986), and particularly Maximé (1986), provide guidance for the translation of theory into practice.

The relationship between white worker and black child can be a powerful experience for both; certainly the two issues of children and race are bound to evoke powerful feelings in the worker. In individual work with children in general there is likely to be a strong identification with the child, and the worker has to separate out and work on 'unfinished business' from his or her own childhood, distinguishing that from what is real for the child in the here-and-now. In direct work with black children, white adults, given the socialization process in which they have been reared, may well have to think very carefully about the implications for themselves and their clients of working with children from different ethnic and racial origins. Nothing can be taken for granted. Cross-cultural work with black children requires white practitioners to address their own ethnicity, and the impact of that on their own sense of self.

An example of this was given by a student in a college sequence addressing 'social work in a multi-racial society'. He spoke about what had been most powerfully evoked for him, namely his own sense of marginality as a young professional from a working-class background. His new social status seemed to his family to be discrepant with his still deeply-held political convictions. He felt that he could no longer legitimately express solidarity with the aspirations of his own group of origin; at the same time, he did not feel wholly at ease with people from well-established middle-class backgrounds.

James Baldwin remarks, 'And anyway the really ghastly thing about trying to convey to a white man the reality of the Negro experience has nothing whatsoever to do with the fact of colour, it has to do with this man's relationship to his own life. He will face in your life only what he is willing to face in his' (Baldwin 1985, p 292). The implication of this is that 'anti-racist training', as it now is, needs both development and differentiation.

Summary

The concept of identity has been used to integrate diverse themes. Social workers constantly encounter people who experience themselves as marginalized or in jeopardy of a split or spoiled identity; the enhancement of self-esteem, therefore, is often postulated as an objective of work undertaken.

In societies which historically have devalued blacks, and developed racial ideologies to justify their subordination, producing the kind of cultural hegemony which purveys negative stereotypes, black children may be prone to the desire to 'be white'. Research findings on the self-concept of black children, from the Forties through to the Eighties, point to difficulties for them in taking themselves for granted in predominantly white groups or communities.

The section on black children in care, in this chapter, addressed issues of identity, *historically* from the stance of reconstituted black families, and *dynamically* with reference to the experiences of black children in the white care-system.

The debate about transracial or same-race placement is essentially a continuation of the debate about what kind of placement is likely to be most conducive to the self-image of a child in need of substitute family care. In the section on direct therapeutic work with black children, it was suggested that issues of identification and identity confront both white workers and black children. This could be a potentially rich and challenging journey, but white workers embarking on a voyage which involves cultural, racial and ethnic identity will certainly need black guides.

7 Creative Direct Work with Adolescents: The Story of Craig Brooks *Miles Hapgood*

Introduction

The direct work bandwagon took some time to reach East Devon, not arriving until 1983. What followed was like a professional version of the playground game, 'British Bulldogs'. One person was 'it' – in our case, the BAAF Regional Coordinator. She had to catch one other person, who was converted to the cause. They then both caught somebody else and so the game continued until the heathens were gradually overwhelmed by the converted. Craig's story, which follows below, explores some of the lessons learnt as these new methods of working were applied to an adolescent in our care.

The term 'direct work' has acquired widespread professional usage but remains somewhat ill-defined. Within our agency it is seen as a means of intervening directly in the lives of children and young people so as to enable them to understand significant events in the past, to confront the feelings engendered by these events, and to become involved more fully in the future planning of their lives. Most practitioners will now have access to training material which explores the theoretical framework of the approach, and the wide range of techniques which have been developed.

Many of these techniques evolved in the course of work with pre-adolescent children awaiting family placement. Their introduction into our agency proved immediately successful, both in terms of the outcome of subsequent placements and in terms of the feedback received from staff using them. However, if used properly, the methods themselves created further organizational challenges. They were particularly time-consuming, often involving two or more members of staff for one half-day each week in preparing and carrying out a programme of work. They required new training in methods and techniques. They only worked effectively within a clear planning context for each child. They involved considerable teamwork from carers, social workers and other professionals, often requiring participants to rethink their professional boundaries. The techniques were emotionally taxing, and staff using them required high levels of supervision and support. Furthermore, the methods were often threatening to those staff whose previous training and experience had been more in looking after children than in working directly with them.

As the methods were successfully applied to work with pre-adolescent children, attention turned to work with adolescents. At that time there were few local developments in the methods used for working with adolescents in care, with the possible exception of some of the assessment techniques being developed within the residential sector. Young people in foster homes or other forms of residential care usually had decisions made about them, rather than *with* them. The main method of intervention, at best, was usually some form of direct personal counselling. Group methods were being developed in the field of intermediate treatment, but with an emphasis more on activity than on addressing the particular forms of behaviour giving cause for concern. Non-verbal methods were rarely used within the agency.

The scope for introducing direct work techniques was considerable, but their introduction proved more difficult with adolescents. Some had been in care for a long time, and both they and their carers had developed relationships which allowed for the avoidance of past pain. Some of the methods, particularly those involving play techniques, were harder to introduce to the older age group. Furthermore, the adolescents were a less passive group to work with; entry into their lives required more direct and challenging negotiation. Despite these practical difficulties, the theoretical base of the direct work model still applied. Adolescents need to understand past events, to deal with feelings which arise from them, and to participate fully in planning about their future.

Craig

I first met Craig in 1984, when he was 15. He had been in care for over 10 years, mainly in a children's home, but also within a foster home and with his father and stepmother. Craig now summarizes his personal history as follows:

The not-so-secret story of Craig Brooks, aged 16¾

My name is Craig and I am 16 years old. I was born on the 18th June 1969 in Exeter. I have a sister Gail who is about two years older than I am, and a brother Neil who is one year younger. My father was a soldier at the time of my birth, and I have been told that I spent some time in Malta but I cannot remember that at all, nor any other part of that life.

When I was about 4½ my mother parted from my father leaving my dad to cope with us three youngsters. My father had to leave the army and he returned to Exeter with us. The going was too tough.

When I was 5 we were put in care. The Social Services put me in a foster home and my brother and sister were also fostered. I was overactive and the foster mother couldn't cope with me.

When I left there I went to live at Colleton Lodge which is an 'all boys' children's home. While I was staying at Colleton Lodge my father met a lovely lady called Linda. They fell in love and married and I went to their wedding and I had a good time.

When I was about 11 years old my brother and I went back to live with Linda and Dad, in a house they rented from the Council. The house we had needed decorating and the garden was full of weeds. We moved in and my brother and I had our own bedroom. My dad bought us new clothes and toys as a getting together present. Linda liked cats so we decided to get one which was a tortoise-shell coloured cat, we named it Tabertha. My sister carried on living with her first foster parents. Every Sunday for the first six months Gail visited us for the day. She stayed for dinner and tea and played games with us. After the six months she rarely came to visit us.

Two years went by and things were wrong. My dad was in the rears with the rent. I was told that I would be going back into care. That day I had the afternoon off school and I went to the Social Services building to see my social worker. When I got there my dad and brother was there and my brother and I was told where we were going. My brother was told that he would be going to Elizabeth Avenue Children's Home and I was going back to Colleton Lodge. I arrived at Colleton Lodge when they were having tea.

While I was staying at Colleton I visited my dad and Linda every Saturday. The secondary school I went to was Priory High School and that's when I started getting interested in computers. The computers they had at school were BBC's Model B and Apple II. My social worker asked me if I was interested in getting fostered. I replied 'yes' and my social worker said that I would be meeting another social worker who helps to find a foster parent for me to stay with.

From Craig's own brief summary of his life history it is obvious that his is not an example of incisive case-planning, although it may not be at all untypical of other cases within other agencies. Indeed Craig's would probably be an all-too-familiar story to researchers like Rowe and Lambert (1973), Shaw and Lebens (1978) and those involved in the recent DHSS-funded research into decision-making in child care (DHSS 1986). Several of the phrases used to describe Craig referred to his early care experiences. He had lost all contact with his mother from an early age (we later found her imprisoned in London), had spent over half his life in a 'boys only' children's home, had experienced many broken promises of rehabilitation or gifts from his father and many changes of social worker during that time. Until more recently there had been little concerted effort to prepare Craig for a future out of care. Despite all this, there was a sense of stability and continuity about Craig's life. He had spent the vast majority of his time in care within a single establishment, where there had been comparatively few changes in children and staff. Furthermore, he had established a pattern of access with some of his family which had endured several years, despite the fact that most professionals involved with Craig felt that he was retaining a hopelessly idealized picture of his father and the promises which he made.

My work with Craig had been agreed contractually with the social workers responsible for him. In considering family placement they had identified certain areas of work which required attention. Four tasks were identified:

– helping Craig to understand his previous life experiences.
– enabling him to learn more about fostering.
– enabling him to consider the most appropriate type of foster family for him.
– enabling him to consider how the other members of his family would react to the proposed family placement.

As well as meeting with Craig's social workers, I met the residential staff caring for him. Craig seemed to evoke a similar response from all those most closely involved with him: a knowing smile and an expression of considerable exasperation. The words used most frequently to describe him included: overactive, insensitive, noisy, computer-mad, friendly, honest, immature, silly, unresponsive. The only two things which seemed important to him were arcade games and his weekly access visit to his father.

Many doubts were expressed about Craig's ability to adapt to family life, even when this was geared towards preparing him for independence. In explaining these doubts, people argued that Craig had been institutionalized during all this time in long-term, unplanned residential care. Behind his open and friendly disposition there seemed to be a lack of any realistic attachment to any adult, a marked absense of any sensitivity to the moods or needs of those around him and an almost obsessive interest in the mechanical world of arcade games. Doubts about family placement were less to do with the management of Craig's adolescent behaviour, and more about the demands on carers caused by Craig's overactivity and the lack of emotional responsiveness he showed to those around him. Residential staff said they could care for him in the knowledge that they would at some point be going off-duty, but how would a foster parent cope?

Initial Planning

The need for some form of life story exercise was self-evident. The file contained no reference to any previous explanatory or counselling work with Craig, and the residential staff themselves were largely unaware of Craig's pre-care experiences. It was felt that, despite the regular contact with his father, Craig had little or no knowledge about his mother, and he was unaware that Gail and himself had different fathers. Various constraints were encountered in planning the life story work. Craig's teachers and residential workers advised that his effective attention span was limited to a few minutes, even in a one-to-one situation. He had some special educational needs which required remedial input from the school. The file contained almost no background information. Craig's father was initially quite receptive to the proposed work, and provided some useful background information. He later found the subjects of our discussions too painful, and withdrew from the work.

I planned to begin with a simple 'year chart' exercise, with the option of then compiling a more detailed life story book based on Craig's occasional interest in photography. This had been encouraged by his school, and one of his teachers offered to supply a camera and assist Craig in developing his own films.

As well as informing Craig about his past, it was hoped that this would evoke some form of emotional response from him, as a starting-point for further work dealing with his self-awareness, and his awareness of those around him. Various techniques were prepared, including the use of feelings cards, the teenager's shield and the ecomap (see Fahlberg 1981b).

Initial thought was also given to Craig's understanding of fostering. His previous personal experience of it had been brief and rejecting, and had occurred some years previously. Although some residents of the children's home had moved to foster parents, the unit had a longer-stay population, and several of the boys had arrived there after disruptions in family placement. It seemed that Craig had little experience of either foster parents or foster children, other than his sister whom he had seen occasionally in the past. We assumed that Craig had only the most limited understanding of fostering and planned for him to meet with experienced foster parents of adolescent children; to visit a past resident of the children's home who was successfully placed with a family; and to participate in functions laid on by the local foster care association.

The Initial Sessions

During the introductory session Craig was clear about my role and could discuss the four agreed tasks. He seemed to accept the family placement plan very readily and was surprised that people should suddenly be taking so much interest in him. Within half an hour he became more tense and fidgety. He introduced his own topics of conversation, almost exclusively about his skill at arcade games which he described in the greatest detail. He also talked randomly about life in the children's home. He responded to questions about his access to his father in neutral terms, and seemed reluctant to take any of this further.

The year chart was introduced for the following two sessions. During the early part of the first session Craig concentrated on his pre-care experiences, revealing many areas of ignorance or uncertainty about his mother, his sister, and the family's travels with the armed forces. Despite this good start, the exercise became heavy going. I had made the fatal mistake of letting Craig know that I owned a home computer myself, and much of the initial sessions were then dominated by Craig's efforts to persuade, cajole or bribe me into lending him this machine.

This ritual would take up a large part of each session, with Craig returning only occasionally to the planned work.

Craig responded more positively to the idea of a photographic life story book, which he viewed as some kind of acceptable project. He made his own arrangements with the school about the use of equipment, and enjoyed the various journeys to places of personal historical note, as well as the attention which he received from everyone whom we saw. He was reintroduced to his sister and learned about his mother's imprisonment in London as a result of alcoholism. This all took place over several weeks, but his interest remained largely factual. At no stage during the life story exercise did Craig show any emotional response to the losses, changes or disappointments which he had experienced.

The introduction of techniques designed to evoke more emotional responses from Craig, and to address his self-awareness, proved difficult from the start. He tolerated the ecomap, but was singularly unimpressed by the teenager's shield. The sessions did enable Craig to share some specific fears to do with darkness and ghosts; these re-emerged after moving to his foster home and were later attributed to his exposure to certain videos whilst with his father. Apart from this, Craig continued to have difficulty in labelling emotions, in understanding the different emotional feelings and responses of those around him (except for the dramatic outbursts of other children in care) and in seeing his family and carers as anything other than constant people around him. This insensitivity made him very vulnerable in a peer group setting, where he was easily controlled by others.

By this time, my own feelings towards Craig began to reflect those of his social worker and carers, which had been vividly described before I started. Whilst Craig enjoyed the company and the attention, he saw less and less relevance in the work that I was asking of him. He began to ask why I would not take him swimming like all his other social workers had done. I felt strong feelings of exasperation, and there were times when I could cheerfully have locked him up permanently inside some arcade machine. I had serious doubts about the realism of the family placement plan.

In talking to Craig later, it transpired that his own feelings were very similar:

> I can't remember much about the early meetings. What I found most interesting was when I was doing the photography bit because then I

was interested in cameras. Miles brought me an album. I don't know if the meetings helped me. I found out some things I didn't know before, like where I was exactly born and about my mother, but I don't think it made much difference. I did not find a flow chart thing very interesting. It wasn't my way of putting things down because I was very into games. That's all I could think about then. I found the ecomap quite boring. I would have liked doing some sort of graph chart showing how much I liked the things around me.

Back to the Drawing Board

We had reached a state of impasse, with all the attendant feelings of disappointment and frustration on my part, and some relief on the part of the existing carers that Craig had not been any different with somebody new. During the summer weeks there had been limited opportunities for individual supervision or group discussion about this piece of work, and this was possibly compounded by a tendency on my part to prefer supervision when all is well.

Supervision, when it did occur, quickly revealed some basic home truths more obvious to those on the outside. While we had negotiated an agenda of work with Craig on a formal level, there was no shared subjective agenda. Insufficient thought had been given to adapting the direct work techniques to Craig's particular strengths and weaknesses. Rather than consider his overriding interest – arcade games – and examine how this could be harnessed, we had regarded this interest as an obstacle to the real job at hand. The reflective opportunities of supervision and group discussion suggested that our attitude to Craig's obsessive interest in arcade games mirrored Craig's own attitude to previous life experiences – ignore it and it might all go away.

Further discussions took place with social workers and residential staff, and it was agreed that Craig should be assisted in buying his own computer. A special room was set aside for him in the children's home, and he borrowed my machine for a few weeks. He created his own personal arcade; he was in paradise.

Miles had a computer himself which was a BBC Micro Model B. He let me borrow his computer for a couple of weeks to try it out as I didn't have one myself. One day after that I was offered a computer which I had to pay at least half towards and the Social Services would pay for the rest. I agreed and in about 2 months I had the money to buy myself a computer. Two weeks passed and I had half a day off school to go shopping. In the end I decided to buy ZX Spectrum 48K and a free game to go with it which cost me £119. I had my own little computer room at Colleton Lodge.

Craig's Programme on Fostering

Craig's main fascination has always been with arcade games, but none of us working with him had properly appreciated his skill in computer programming. Although well below the average academically, and despite very little opportunity to practise on his own, Craig soon showed some natural flair and ability in basic computer programming.

After some time spent together working on the programming possibilities of Craig's new machine, I toyed with the idea of asking Craig to construct a simple game about his care experiences (*Trapped in Care* or *Alien from the Social Services* etc.). Craig came up with an alternative idea – a programme to help children or young people who might be fostered. Craig describes his work on this below:

Miles came to see me again and we talked about if I would like to write a programme for him to do with fostering. I agreed and we sat down talking about what we wanted in the programme. We wanted to have questions for children to answer to help find a suitable home for the child. The sort of questions I was thinking of was, Do you think your parents are happy that you are being fostered? What interest would you like to share with them?

I did a programme with an introduction and then 4 stages. Between each stage I wrote graphics in the programme so it was not too boring. I did things like a sunset and a jogger moving across the screen. I copied some of these in from magazines.

At the start of the programme there was some sound effects and the letters in 'FOSTERING' came up one by one on the screen. Then there were the instructions which looked like this:

FOSTERING – A Programme for the Social Services

This is a programme for you if you might be fostered.
You will be asked questions in 4 stages. Please answer in short sentences or single words. I you don't want to answer questions or it doesn't apply, type a 'O'. You can either do it by yourself or with someone to help you.

Your answers are being stored in the computer. Contact the person in charge when you have finished.

Copyright Craig Brooks

****

The person was then asked simple questions like, What is your Name?
What is Your Age? Where are you Living? What is your Mother's Name?
What is your Father's Name? and the same for brothers and sisters. After some more graphics the screen showed:

STAGE 1 - FOSTERING AND YOU

The questions come onto the screen one at a time. They changed when the person pressed the return key. The questions in Stage 1 were:

Have you ever been fostered before?
If yes, did you like the people you were with?
How long did you stay there?
Why did you leave them?
Do you know anyone else who has been fostered?
What is his or her name?
Is he or she still with his or her foster parents?
Is he or she enjoying it there?
Do you think fostering is for you?

STAGE 2 - FOSTERING AND YOUR FAMILY

The letters were in different colours and then there were these questions:

In a few minutes there will be a list of names and I would like you to put how often you would like to see them – i.e. never, weekly, monthly etc.

Father
Mother
Sisters
Brothers
Aunts
Uncles
Grandparents

If we have not mentioned anyone important to you please tell us his or her name and how often you want to see him or her.

Do you think your parents are happy that you are being fostered?

STAGE 3 - WHICH FOSTER PARENTS

The questions here were:
What sort of people do you want to live with?
What interests would you like them to have?
Do you want other children in the house?
Do you want to share a room with anyone?
What else would you like to say about foster parents?

STAGE 4 - MEETING FOSTER PARENTS

The questions I asked were:
Where would you like to meet them?
How many times would you like to see them so you can decide if you want to stay with them?
How long would you like to stay with them so you can decide if you want to stay there?
Are there any other questions you would like to ask?

That was the end of the programme. They were told to call the person in charge. There was a code which you could use to get all the answers back on the screen so you could talk about them. The programme could be used with either a tape recorder or a disc drive.

The questions I had wrote for the programme helped me to think more about fostering and what it was like. At the beginning I thought fostering was where the child is dumped into somebody's home for six months and if they liked they stayed and if they didn't they went to a new place. But now I think it is more caring, they don't tell where you are going to go but instead they ask what sort of parents you like, and what hobbies you like etc. The Social Services don't rush you to make your mind up about things like if you would like to stay with somebody for the weekend, or ask you would you like to live with them now? Instead they take things slowly, you decide with the foster parent and the social worker when it is convenient for you to go and visit the foster parent.

Craig moved to his foster family six months after I met him, and after a six week introduction. At the time of writing he had been there over two years. Initially, some of our worst fears were realised. He seemed to view the family as a smaller-scale children's home, preferable mainly because there were fewer formal restrictions. Since then there has been a slow, sometimes comic and sometimes painful process of integration into family life, from which he will soon be preparing for some form of independent living. This process can be traced in Craig's own account of his experiences within the family, excerpts from which are set our below:

> During when we were discussing the programme Miles said that he has found a foster parent which is interested in fostering me. Her name was Eileen. We decided to go and see Eileen for a cup of tea and I met Helen and Jeremy (Eileen's grown up children). I stayed with them for about an hour and talked about staying at her house for a weekend. Before I met Eileen and her family I was a bit nervous, questions were going through my head what sort of family were they. What would they think of me. What sort of computer Jeremy had. When I met them I was happy to be with them because they seemed to be very nice people. I left about four and went back to Colleton and told Aunty June what they were like. By now me and Miles had finished discussing about the programme and I sat down with his computer and started writing it. After about three weeks it was finished. There was two versions of the programme one with graphics in and other with no graphics . . .
>
> I decided with Eileen that I would visit for the weekend. The weekend went well and I enjoyed it. There was good things like I enjoyed it because the atmosphere was much different than living at Colleton Lodge. The time I went to bed was much different, at Colleton I had to be in bed by a certain time but at Eileen's I can go to bed when I like . . .
>
> Eileen arranged for me to have new glasses because the old glasses were national health glasses and they didn't make me look smart. My new glasses had reactolite lenses with gold rims. I had some new clothes and I had a crew cut. At Eileen's I had a lot more freedom to go where I wanted to go as long as I told Eileen where I was going and what time I would be back. Jeremy's friend came round to the house and played games on the computer. My friends came round as well to play on my games . . .
>
> At carnival time Eileen's Sunday School had a float in the procession and I helped to collect money for charity. I looked after a

young girl called Wanda who helped to collect money. At the end of the Carnival me and Wanda got lost so we had to walk home and I had to carry her because she was tired . . .

At Christmas I stayed with Eileen from Christmas Eve; the family always go to church at midnight and so I went with them. After church we drank punch and I had mince pies before we went to bed. I spent Christmas Day with Dad and Linda and on Boxing Day with Eileen's family and everyone who came in. Among my presents I had a joystick and interface for my computer and some games . . .

This year I spent Christmas with Eileen and on Boxing Day I stayed with Dad. As usual the family were at Eileen's including Emily, Helen's baby who was born 6th December. New Year's Eve I went to a disco, I had a good time . . .

Back to college in the New Year then at Easter Eileen's grandson David was christened at West Wycombe, we went down in the coach and I met Eileen's mum and dad, they are old and I did not know what they would think of me. I stayed at the home of a friend of Eileen's. After the service we went to Stephen's home and we had a family get together. We came home on Easter Monday and Eileen told me that her parents like me!

Evaluation

The use of the computer proved immeasurably more successful than any of the methods attempted previously in helping Craig understand the transition from residential care to family placement. It seemed to help Craig think himself into a new situation, and also provided him with a sense of control and choice over what was happening to him, although occasionally he would find the responsibilities of choosing very difficult to deal with. He was keen that the programme should have some practical use. As part of the preparation process we visited a foster home where Craig used the programme with a youngster already placed. This was a significant event for Craig, since the programme was well received by everybody within the foster family. We also introduced it to another residential setting where some children were prepared for family placement.

Despite all this, the work undertaken with Craig was only partially successful in terms of the original goals. In particular, we made only limited progress in enhancing his emotional development, and in allowing him to explore his feelings of previous events and his attachments to those around him. This sense of failure may be due more to the expectations we set ourselves than the techniques which we employed. Greater realism about the extent of Craig's previous emotional deprivation was needed, since no method can get to emotions and feelings which have never properly developed. However, by the end of the sessions we were able to provide prospective foster parents with a more realistic assessment about Craig's needs, and this did help Eileen with her personal expectations of Craig after placement.

In evaluating this work, we were struck by how our enthusiasm for applying new techniques took us away from some basic social work principles. Text-book phrases about 'shared agendas', 'starting where the client is' and 'the reflective use of supervision' are well illustrated in this process. No social work method can be too prescriptive – they all require careful adaptation to the circumstances of each child and young person, and this is especially true of direct work methods. In retrospect, much of the work with Craig now seems unsophisticated, a reflection of the considerable progress made more recently in developing better techniques for working with adolescents. Furthermore, as the range of direct work methods increases, so does the range of new techniques being used in other aspects of child care work, as seen in the treatment of sexual abuse, in community assessment programmes and in diversionary schemes for young people facing care or custody. Similar to direct work, these methods have been developed within specialist settings, often involving other disciplines. There are some areas of overlap, but also new skills in group work, individual counselling and behaviour-focussed programmes. For those of us involved in the development of child care services within Social Services Departments, the need for some integration of all these techniques and ideas represents the next challenge. 1983 already seems a long time ago.

8 Meeting the Needs of Workers

*Eva Banks and Sarah Mumford, with an introduction by
John Simmonds*

Supervision in social work occupies a paradoxical position, for while on
the one hand it figures highly on the agendas of almost all social
workers as a necessary part of good practice, recent research evidence
(Vernon and Fruin 1985, Rowlands 1983 and Parsloe 1981) suggests
that it is infrequent and often unsatisfactory in content, and that it
provides social workers with little opportunity to systematically plan
and review their work. The reasons for this are complex. Supervision as
an activity has always been difficult because of its dual role: facing the
organization on the one hand, with its demand for control and
accountability; facing workers on the other, with their need for
support, direction and professional development. If the focus of
supervision is one problem, its dynamics and processes are another,
with its capacity to stir up issues concerning authority and dependency
(Mattison and Sinclair 1979, Mattinson 1975, Dearnley 1985). While
there have been developments in the area of supevision in recent years
(Gambrill and Stein 1978, Atherton 1986, Collins and Bruce, 1984) it is
clear that in many respects it still poses major problems both for
departments and for individual social workers.

Given the issues reviewed in Chapter 1 concerning the lack of visiting
of children in care and the lack of knowledge about them (see
Blom-Cooper 1985), one can only assume that the supervision of social
workers undertaking any kind of direct work with children is woefully
inadequate. Yet, as has been pointed out in many examples in this
book, the stress placed on social workers when working with children is
very high and they have a corresponding need for support and
professional consultation. Resolving the conflict between the pressure
to become emotionally available to the child and the need to retain
objectivity and a clear sense of personal and professional boundaries is

difficult. This is particularly so in the case of the interaction of feelings in the professional relationship, and the capacity of these feelings to evoke patterns reminiscent of earlier relationships in the child's life. In these situations, it is the capacity of the worker to find an emotional space in the mind able to tolerate these feelings that is critical to the child's feeling understood. If this is so for the worker it is also true for the supervisor. As Hoxter says,

> We require to be vigilant that our receptivity is not being impaired by these defenses and that we too are not drawn into playing a part in the 'cycle of deprivation' despite our firmest intentions to offer a relationship which provides a path out of the cycle. (Hoxter 1983, p 126)

In the following account, Eva Banks and Sarah Mumford describe their experiences in developing supervision for social workers working directly with children.

The Setting

The current climate in many social services departments is often not helpful in facilitating innovations in social work practice, because of the competing demands of pressures of time and of too many cases in need of urgent allocation. As a team leader and a social worker in an Inner London Social Services Department's children's team, we have experienced these pressures and recognised that direct work with children brings its own additional demands, as outlined in Chapter 1.

Direct work with children requires a high level of commitment from all those involved, and this must include supervision as a regular and integral part of its framework. In addition, there has to be some acknowledgement within the agency of the value of work with children, and hence agreement for spending money on toys and equipment such as books, dolls, clay, and plastic telephones. Most workers will build up their own 'kit' and be happy to add to this as their experience grows. Training and consultation are also resources that must be available. We do realise that we cannot assume these to be regular features in all agencies, but they must be fought for as a baseline: without them, working with children becomes impossible, as there is no framework within which to seek support.

Beginnings

Given a supportive and encouraging supervisory relationship, workers need to evaluate their current level of knowledge and skills. Sarah describes her beginning in the children's team:

> I was new to the team and to my supervisor. My caseload was gradually building up and I had a host of new things to get used to: new colleagues, office, clients and above all children! I had little experience of working directly with children and felt a lack of a working knowledge of child care legislation. It was essential for me to have a supervisor who knew her way around the law and whose experience on child care was extensive. I knew that Eva was very interested and involved in using play as a work method with children but, in my first few months, I used supervision to focus on getting an understanding and basic knowledge in child care. Without this, I would have lacked the basis on which to build my work.

When the worker feels ready to undertake work with children, the first step will be the hardest, as in any new venture. Even experienced workers will ask: 'Where do I start? What toys will I need? What should I say? How do I explain what we will be doing? How should I structure the first session? What if we run out of things to do? How long should the first session be? What if I make an idiot of myself?'

Our experience is that it is best to deal with such questions as directly and openly as possible. Careful planning of, and preparation for, the first session pays dividends, not least in giving the worker some reassurance and confidence. The worker needs to explain to the child *why* they will be meeting, how often and where. It may be helpful to rehearse the approach in supervision: 'We are going to have a special time each week on a Tuesday . . . we'll play and have some fun but we'll also do some work sorting out all the places where you've lived . . . preparing for your new family . . . doing your life story book . . .' It is also useful to anticipate what toys the particular child may respond to initially, according to age, temperament and interests (see West 1983). If the workers are not using an equipped playroom then they need to have a travelling kit of toys. Generally, for younger children some soft toys, some small figures, one or two puppets, two toy telephones (because some children find it difficult to talk about painful issues face to face), some paper and crayons will provide a good basis for the first few sessions.

The first session with the child should set the framework, taking into account the assessment made and its objectives (see Chapter 2). The room and toys should be explored; things to do in the future should be planned. For example, are the worker and child going to share some food and a drink? (Haworth and Keller 1964). At what point during each session will this take place? It may also be appropriate for the worker and child to acknowledge their apprehension – it will be the first time they have met for 'special' sessions.

The first child Sarah assessed for direct work was a four year old boy called John, who had been recently orphaned and received into care. There had been some concern about the extent to which John had been given the opportunity by the adults in his life to mourn his mother – an issue discussed extensively by Jewett (1984). Sarah was aware that the work would be painful, challenging and possibly personally threatening, as she would be putting herself in touch with a child's world, and hence with her own childhood and the child within herself.

> At the beginning of our first supervision session Eva asked me what I wanted to achieve. I started with only a vague notion that here was a child in pain who needed to know that it was not his fault his mother had died, and that it was safe to express his anger, but I was unsure whether it was possible for me to help him to do this through play. I needed to know just how to begin, what materials to take with me, how often to visit and how to include the foster parents.
>
> In discussion with Eva we decided that I should provide John with a bag of knitted dolls which he could use to help him express his feelings about his family. I made it clear to him from the beginning that I had brought these dolls especially for him. It took no encouragement for him to take out of the bag each doll, one by one, carefully looking at them and spontaneously identifying each one as 'Mummy', 'the doctor', 'John' (himself) and so on. The first sessions were spent with the 'Mummy' doll and 'John' doll locked in close embrace, alternately hiding from each other then being reunited and all the other dolls firmly put away or hidden. During this, Sarah sat listened and repeated back some of what John said, sometimes asking a question for clarification, occasionally offering a suggestion.
>
> In supervision we discussed what we thought would be some of the major concerns for John – loss, separation and death. We were aware that John could be very worried that his mother's death had

something to do with him (see Jewett 1984, Fahlberg 1981b), thinking perhaps that she had died because he had been 'naughty'. We felt that he needed to know the facts – that the hospital and the doctors had tried to make her better but that she was too ill.

Having anticipated this, at an appropriate time in the next session I introduced the subject of the doctor. I told John that the doctor had tried to make his mother better in the hospital and how sad the doctor was when he was not able to do so. John took up this theme immediately and began to enact the scene at the hospital with the doctor doll operating on the 'Mummy' doll. When the doctor doll 'failed' in his task, it became the object of all John's anger, and he would receive severe reprimands for not making people better. John would end one of these conversations by giving the 'doctor' doll a punch in the face or by holding the doll's legs and bashing the doll against the floor.

At the end of this session, John put the dolls back into their bag, leaving 'Mummy' doll' to the last, when he would tenderly caress and kiss the doll before gently returning it to the bag.

Although the 'doctor' doll came in for almost constant abuse from John, there came a time when he expressed his anger towards the 'Mummy' doll by tying it up to a stick with yards of string, dragging it around the floor like a dog on a lead. At the end of this session, when it came to putting the dolls away John gave the 'Mummy' doll a quick kiss and hastily put it into the bag with all the other dolls.

The intensity of John's aggression towards the 'Mummy' doll on this occasion was never repeated, and in subsequent sessions 'Mummy' doll was cared for, hidden away or kissed lovingly while the 'doctor' doll received John's anger.

We had anticipated that at some point John would express anger towards his mother for 'leaving him' and that it was important that he was not prevented from getting angry with her. He needed to know that it was safe to have angry feelings. He also needed to know that his mother did not want to die, that she wanted to stay alive and look after John, and that it made her very sad that her body was sick and she wanted to get better.

Throughout the work with John we continually discussed the content of the sessions and tried to identify the themes that he was presenting. Although we had not set a fixed time-scale for this work with John, recognising that he needed to work at his own pace, we were also aware of the need to set some limit to it and to plan for its end. When we felt reasonably sure, through observing John's behaviour and discussing this with his foster parents, that he had made some progress in resolving his feelings about his mother's death, we planned to bring the work to a close. In one particular session John did not play with the dolls but merely checked that each one was present and returned them all to the bag. On my last visit to John he said goodbye to each doll, deliberately and slowly, and for the last time kissed the 'Mummy' doll and the 'John' doll, placing them in the bag together!

Supervision is essential in enabling the worker to cope with the intensity of the feelings raised, for example, by working with a bereaved child. If Sarah had not used supervision in this way she might have become overwhelmed. Eva was aware of the risks of exposing inexperienced workers to such powerful feelings. In an ideal world she would not have chosen a bereaved child for any worker to begin direct work. However there is rarely ever the luxury of choice, and although John was very sad, very shocked and very angry, he had received good and consistent care from his mother before her death. In consequence he had a good sense of self, which would help him begin to cope with his loss. The alacrity with which he responded to the sessions was reassuring. He clearly found his relationship with Sarah strong and safe enough for him to express his feelings.

John had to know that it was permissible to talk about his Mummy and to be sad and angry that she had died. If Eva and Sarah could bear the pain of their feelings about John's bereavement in supervision, then Sarah could gain the confidence to deal with John's feelings, as well as her own, in her sessions with him.

While the direct work with John was of central importance to him at that particular moment in time, helping children to cope with experiences of loss must happen within the context of establishing a child in a secure and long-term family placement, as discussed in Chapter 3. Supervisors must not therefore become diverted, in focussing on the immediacy of direct work sessions, from ensuring that a clear goal exists for the child, and that this plan is implemented.

Supervisors also need to inform themselves sufficiently about the range of techniques available so that they can suggest alternative and perhaps unconventional approaches to direct work. This may, for example, sometimes mean being flexible and imaginative about where the child is seen by the worker. For example, at the time of writing,

Lennox is a difficult and exhausting seven year old. He has a history of neglect and probable sexual abuse. Sarah had tried to work with Lennox in his cramped bedroom. Not surprisingly this was unsatisfactory. She sensed that Lennox needed space but could not think how to create it. Eva and Sarah discussed this in supervision together and agreed that the pressure of the current arrangement was not helping Lennox. When they were also able to recognize that Sarah was fearful about failing with him, it then became possible for them to think about planning the sessions in a more suitable way, and they agreed that she would take him to the park once a week. Now she cannot stop Lennox talking!

Implications for the Supervisor

Developing supervisory skills in new areas of practice can be daunting for even the most experienced senior worker. Dearnley (1985) provides a useful guide to the complex processes by which people learn to be supervisors. We have drawn on some of her ideas in looking at supervision in relation to direct work with children. In the same way that social workers cannot isolate themselves from the impact of children's feelings, supervisors must also feel safe enough to recognize the impact of the feelings that can be stirred up in them during supervision. It can be easy for supervisors to feel de-skilled, excluded from and envious of the special relationship that develops between social worker and child, and the development of the new skills acquired in the process. If these feelings come to dominate the supervisor and he or she then feels defensive about his or her lack of knowledge or experience, the relationship and the supervisor's usefulness to the worker can become diminished. Supervisors need to develop their own support networks, which will include other professionals, and learn to draw on their own internal sense of being good enough as a supervisor. Dearnley (1985) believes that only by doing this can there be any 'development of a sense of credibility of supervisory competence and confidence, so that there is a freedom "not to know" and to be more open by imaginative association to the worker's explicit and implicit material. Then, hopefully one discovers one's own style, becomes comfortable with it, and creates and refines a framework of knowledge in which to operate'.

107

The Supervisory Process

Inevitably, the relationship between each supervisor and supervisee is unique, but there are common general themes. Individual needs and personalities shape the sessions. The tone and tenor will be determined by different cases at different times, by personal preoccupations and agency demands and requirements, but at the same time there are parts of the process which are universal. When supervision sessions are supportive, creative, imaginative and humorous, then this will contribute to the worker's confidence.

The emotional atmosphere of the supervision sessions is particularly important, not just because it provides support for the worker, but also because it can be a means of understanding the work with the child. Mattinson (1975, Mattinson and Sinclair 1979) uses the term 'the reflection process' to describe her understanding of the way that unresolved or uncontained feelings between a worker and an adult client can become reenacted in the relationship between worker and supervisor. This concept has helped us to understand similar issues in working with children. It was highlighted for us when Sarah was working with James, age 13. For weeks we ploughed through supervision sessions, trying to understand him and some of his difficulties. Eva felt that she just could not get to grips with him and Sarah seemed depressed and despairing about him, convinced she would never get anywhere. She writes:

James had been in care nearly all his life and had had numerous changes of placement. He was an unhappy child who looked and behaved much younger than his age. The staff at his children's home found him hard to understand and difficult to contain. As a worker visiting him once a fortnight I found the task of developing any kind of relationship with him almost impossible. When I visited James he would rarely look at me or say anything and was always firmly ensconced in front of the television as soon as he was home from school.

This experience came to dominate supervision, with Sarah finding that she had little to say to Eva. The sessions themselves seemed unproductive. The breakthrough in supervision coincided with a breakthrough in the work. Sarah and James went out together and bought some hamburgers. He would not eat them anywhere but back in the children's home, where he clearly enjoyed the attention of Sarah and two female members of staff. The description of James, brought to supervision, sitting on the adults' knees in turn, drinking from each of their coffee cups, revealed the toddler that was struggling to get out of this now 14 year old body. Once Eva and Sarah understood James's basic need for attention and comfort, it became possible to think of an appropriate programme for him. The first work focussed on the senses, and involved games based on taste, smell, touch, sound and sight. James began to enjoy his sessions thoroughly and they became very important to him. Our knowledge and understanding of James grew and our supervisions took on a new lease of life.

Organisation and Management of Workload

If a worker is to undertake work with a child on a regular weekly or fortnightly basis then it is vital that account be taken of preparation time, supervision time and the drain on emotional, intellectual and physical resources. Seeing a child on a regular basis often involves work at the end of the day after school, and there is a limit not only to the amount of time available for this kind of commitment, but also the energy required to share play activities at this level with a child, as well as meeting the demands of the job as a whole. The stress on a worker can be considerable as the numbers of children in care who need direct work becomes apparent. Decisions then need to be made about which children to work with.

There has to be an honest discussion about how much time each case requires, what tasks need to be done and what things can be delayed. We operate a system of workload management and, although there is a groan once a quarter when the forms appear, it is nevertheless a very helpful exercise which measures how much time a caseload needs, and shows the pressure points. The exercise affords a useful review of the workload, and Eva and Sarah will discuss in fairly practical terms which children need direct work and what help foster parents and families require. Decisions need to be made about priorities and this does require a discipline in determining objectives, and a clarity about purpose.

Our feeling is that the need for direct work with children is matched by the need for both supervisors and agencies to find ways of meeting the supervision and training requirements of workers. In the current climate this can often seem like one more demand following so many others. However, our experience suggests, without any doubt, that such attention not only goes a long way towards tackling some of the urgent needs of children in care, but also does much to raise the professional morale of those involved in planning for or directly meeting these needs.

9 Introducing Direct Work with Children to Area Teams in Social Services Departments *Eve Hopkirk*

Introduction

In the busy district office in which I work, I was aware of a few social workers using life story books on a similar basis to myself. I thought it likely that they would welcome opportunities to learn new ways of working with children. I also thought there might be pockets of expertise within the office which were not being tapped and from which others could learn. It seemed logical and natural to combine and learn together from each other. My method was therefore to organise and run a training group of social work colleagues with the aim of increasing our skills, knowledge and sensitivity in direct work and communication with children.

Setting Up and Forming the Group

With the support of senior management, I decided to offer eight sessions for a total of eight social workers including myself. I thought this number would allow the group sufficient opportunity to form itself as an entity. As the nature of the subject was likely to evoke strong emotions, linked with childhood memories and experiences, I thought that the group should consist of no more than eight people. Group members selected themselves on a first come, first served basis.

Preparation

Preparation took four main forms:

1 An initial planning meeting.
2 Acquiring a knowledge base from reading and from Goldsmiths' course material.

3 Consultations with experienced social workers.
4 Developing self-awareness.

1 The Planning Meeting

This was arranged with group members to clarify the aim of the group, which was for all its members to acquire new skills and knowledge about direct work and communication with children. It was also necessary to clarify my role. Should I draw up the agenda or should this come from the group? Should we involve outsiders with specialist skills in one or two sessions, bearing in mind the impact that outsiders can make on a group? We established that my role should be that of catalyst or facilitator; I should draw up an agenda on which the group could base its work and, far from being a problem, the input from outside experts would be warmly welcomed.

2 Acquiring a Knowledge Base

A major source of help to me in preparing for the group were the experiential sessions in direct work with children demonstrated and led by Nessie Bailey at Goldsmiths' College. I was able to consolidate and expand on this teaching in the two months between the planning meeting and the group's first session. Oaklander (1978), Jewett (1984) and the BAAF training pack *In Touch with Children* (1984) were of particular help.

3 Consultation with Experienced Workers

I consulted two experienced social workers. The first showed me an example of a life story book. I also saw the suitcase of toys and other materials with which this social worker travels. I learnt of all the preliminary work which has to be done with children before reaching the point when they are ready for life story books. I began to see areas of work with children on which I could concentrate and learn, so that my task seemed more manageable.

From meeting a second worker, I was made aware of the vast range of skills, techniques and knowledge which exist to help children understand themselves and their past. I realised, too, that all the techniques, such as posters, life trees, life roads, and the teenagers' shield, have grown from the imagination of social workers trying to find

112

ways of conveying ideas and information to children, and help them formulate and express their wishes and feelings. I realised that in my own imagination I might have a resource with which I could help children in the future.

Developing Self-Awareness

From the earliest days of thinking about setting up the group, I found myself frequently wishing to abandon it, as not only the method but the subject matter seemed too difficult. However, this changed quite dramatically after my reading of two papers by Winnicott (1986) and Curtis (1981). Winnicott impressed me with her crisis intervention approach in childhood to forestall emotional disabilities in adult life (see Chapter 3). To this Curtis adds:

> we must be prepared to seek contact with the suffering part of the child in order to help him overcome the pain and give him the stability which can help him face the future. If we do not help the child to face the pain, he will never be able to reach his potential for living and relating to the world. (Curtis 1981, p 16)

I realised then that I was running away from the pain of children and that, if I could not face that, I would never be able to help a child to do so. I considered also that in this might lie at least a partial and possible explanation for the comparative lack of attention given to this work: the pain of children is so distressing and disturbing to adults that it is very much easier to devote our energies to working around them than to working directly with them. This realisation enabled me to concentrate wholeheartedly on the preparation for the group, and the subject matter on which it was to focus.

Overview of the Content of Material Used by the Group as a Basis for the Work

I found that I had begun to probe a vast subject of which I had previously been unaware. I wanted to select those parts which I thought would be most useful, relevant, interesting and important, on which the group could focus as the agenda for our eight weekly sessions.

Agenda

Session 1	Facing the pain of children
	Beginning work with a child
	Casework principles
	Brainstorming – building trust
	Experiential work: Take your pencil for a walk
	Family drawings
Session 2	Child development
	Slides
	Quiz
	Guided fantasy
Session 3	Separation
	Bereavement
	Flow charts
	Painting feelings
Session 4	Attachment
Session 5	Helping children understand their past
	Life story books, flow charts, etc.
Session 6	Helping the 'emotionally stuck' child
	The loving and caring water technique
	The loving and caring candle technique
Session 7	Play therapy
Session 8	Helping children with anger

The Content of the Sessions

In the space permitted, it is impossible to describe each session fully. I propose to discuss the first and the last in detail and indicate the main features of the remainder.

Session 1

At the start of the group, there was an atmosphere of expectancy and some nervousness, the latter largely my own. Children's toys, books and posters were displayed to remind the group of childhood. This provoked lively comments. I had planned a packed programme of work for the group – a common mistake made by novice group workers (Douglas 1976). After preliminary discussions related to the organisation of the group, I outlined what was on offer. I had some skills and knowledge to give the group but other members also had similar resources on which it could draw. I emphasised that this was *their* group, to be used for learning as members wanted.

To start the discussion, I stated our objective of wanting to learn more about direct work with children, and my growing conviction of its importance. I referred to the need to face children with their pain and grief and the potential damage to them involved in avoiding this. Lively discussions followed. One group member spoke of the dilemma of trying to help a distressed child when the social worker himself was apparently responsible for causing the suffering. A child client of his was distressed by not seeing his father. The social worker attempted to deal with this, knowing that he himself had been much involved in the decision to stop the father's access, thereby increasing the distress. Several group members identified with this. One had been faced with the dilemma of moving a little girl from one foster home to the only available alternative, although he knew this was not a suitable placement for her. Both group members felt guilty about matters for which they were not entirely responsible. The reasons for stopping access lay in the father's behaviour and were therefore his responsibility while inadequate resources were responsible for the lack of choice of foster home. Other group members voiced their fears of working with children – fear of damaging the child by tampering in areas in which they had little expertise, and fear of being unable to handle certain feelings aroused. These were my worries too at the beginning of the project.

The group did not resolve these problems, but avoided them, thus reflecting a common tendency in us all to circumvent the pain of children. I should have pointed this out to the group, but only realised in retrospect what had taken place. Instead, the group turned to an animated (and safer) discussion of casework principles and brainstorming ways of building trust with children.

Two experiential exercises followed. The first – 'Take your pencil for a walk' (Winnicott 1984) – provoked hilarity, but the group appreciated its use in engaging a child and encouraging communication, and as a projection tool. I then invited the group to draw their family members either as animals or symbols (Oaklander 1978). When I first experienced this exercise, I was amazed at the vividness with which perceptions and feelings can be conveyed by it. One group member represented his mother as a large house and the ground underneath. He told us of her solidity and reliability, her great importance to his family.

His father was drawn as the study where he spent much time and was inaccessible to the family. A bird 'flying around' was his brother, who is unsettled in various areas of his life, and a tortoise the group member himself because, although slow, he 'gets there in the end'. Two group members did not want to reveal themselves in this way and this was accepted by the group.

I gave the group a case illustration of the use of family drawings. This is a techique by which children are encouraged to express their feelings by pretending that they and their families are different animals. Children choose what they want everyone to be. They draw the animals and make them talk to each other. Often a child who finds it difficult to talk about relationships directly can use this imaginative play to advantage.

At the end of the session the group seemed subdued. I commented on this. One group member related it to the pain of children, while another said the session had been like a holiday and he was reluctant to return to work. I added that the last exercise might have touched some sad feelings and memories of the past.

Session 2

My intention was to offer this session as an opportunity for the group to revise its knowledge of child development in order to enable members to assess the developmental level of any child with whom they might work closely. I borrowed slides (the kind used for training health visitors) to remind the group of the developmental changes which a normal child undergoes. I also gave them references to texts on child development (Sheridan 1986, Cooper 1986). I devised a short quiz on emotional and linguistic development so as to remind the group of these areas. It included posters and leaflets to set the scene. I planned to talk about 'emotionally damaged' children. I read widely, and felt competent to teach. I also looked at work on children's sensory development (Cooper 1986). The realisation that many children in care have senses which are so undeveloped as to be almost atrophied, provoked some interest. This grew when I invited group members to feel, smell and taste an orange and other objects. A relaxed and humorous atmosphere developed. However, my contention that we had a duty to stimulate the senses of children to compensate them for what they had missed was greeted with some scepticism. Interestingly, this had also been my initial reaction to these ideas.

116

To end this session, I gave the group an opportunity to test the technique of 'guided fantasy'. This is a method used to help individuals explore the content of their imagination. For further discussion of this see Oaklander (1978, p 3). Oaklander recommends that group members draw what they have seen at the end of their journey, in 'their space', at the end of the 'fantasy trip'. Our group was enthusiastically absorbed in this for about fifteen minutes. They were amazed at the results. One person drew a stretch of a river familiar to her, to which she and her husband frequently went before he died. Another had seen his prep school. A third drew a room with a welcoming fire and a pot plant, while a fourth had seen and heard a room full of music, the notes of which she drew vividly. These four people took their drawings with them. The remainder, including myself, who had either not been able to relax sufficiently, and saw nothing, or pretended to see something they had not, left theirs behind.

Session 3

Attendance slumped in the following meeting, though for ostensibly good reasons, and apologies for absence were given. Its theme was separation and bereavement. I found Jewett's work (1984) helpful here, particularly the fourth chapter, 'Making Sense of Loss'. Despite the smaller membership, the session went well. The group did an exercise (Fahlberg 1981b, p 36) in which members imagined themselves as separated children and brainstormed the feelings this aroused. There was general recognition that these were the feelings and reactions of well-attached children. This led to a discussion of the range of children's reactions to separation and the factors affecting them. One group member spoke of two children with whom he is working who showed no emotional response at their second foster home disruption, and then 'jumped all over' the officer in charge on first meeting him at the children's home to which they moved.

After discussion of the stages of bereavement (Bowlby 1980) and the use of crisis theory to build trust at points of separation (see Chapter 3), I showed the group Jewett's list of five needs which children must satisfy if they are to recover fully from a loss.

First the child must understand that he was born to a mother and father, he must know who they were and why he was separated from one or both of them . . . Second, the child must know what persons or families have cared for him if he has lived away from his first parents . . . Third, the child must say goodbye, directly or symbolically, to past caretakers (and if a change of caretaker is forthcoming, he must say hello to the new caretaker). Fourth, the child must receive permission from his caretakers to be happy, loved, successful and loving. Fifth, the child must get ready to face the future with increasingly diminishing concern about the past. (Jewett 1984, 129–30).

In the discussion of flow charts which followed, a group member who has a scientific background declared her dislike of them. However, as she worked on hers, she recalled with some feeling two major losses in her life and thus came to an appreciation of their potential in helping children understand, and grieve, their losses.

Session 4

For this session, I involved two group members in the presentation of material on attachment; one of them had knowledge of Bowlby's work (Bowlby 1961, 1973 and 1980) and the other of Fahlberg's writing (1981a). This proved an enjoyable and productive way of learning together.

Sessions 5 and 6

These were also extremely valuable. Many children find difficulty in making attachments to new families and retaining appropriate feelings for their past carers (Jenkins 1981). Jewett (1984), Fahlberg (1981b) and Owen and Curtis (1983) all describe the technique of using the 'loving and caring candle' as a symbolic way of showing children that they need not stop loving one caretaker in order to love another. This is a powerful and emotionally touching exercise, and a very important one to learn. Because these techniques can have such an impact upon worker and child, it is important that workers know what they are doing. As Owen and Curtis warn,

> We have been concerned that some of the techniques have been subsequently applied by some workers without their fully understanding the implications for the child. Applying half-learned ideas can further damage children and it is vital to have enough background knowledge and experience in this work to be able to deal with the stress and emotions that are evoked. (Owen and Curtis 1983, p 1)

Because of this warning, I found it helpful to have the support of experienced workers throughout the two sessions, to teach the group the correct way to apply the various techniques.

Session 7

In this seventh meeting, on play therapy, one group member outlined the principle of non-directive play (Axline 1947). She illustrated this with an account of her work with a ten year old boy. The group was very interested and impressed by the potential of this work and linked it to the use of free play in assessing children's attachments, discussed in the sixth session.

Session 8

This final session, which was on helping children with anger, is described in more detail as an illustration of the last and the best of the group's work. The session started with one member seeking and obtaining ideas for work which he wished to undertake with a child. The group was very sensitive, supportive and sympathetic to him when he revealed his uncertainties and fears. The group discussed the concept of anger and, at my suggestion, did an exercise to increase awareness of their own and other people's anger. They settled down to the task with great concentration, and discussed the attitudes and feelings which the exercise revealed. The common response was fear in the face of anger. The group as a whole drew strength from knowing that they were not alone in this feeling.

We discussed the influence of culture and family on the ways in which people handle their anger (Jewett 1984), and the problems adults often have in allowing children to express theirs. Adult reactions often encourage children to feel shame and guilt, causing them to suppress their feelings. In addition, children are often afraid to be angry for fear of annoying adults. Some fear the power and damaging potential of these feelings. Others fear that loss of control damages themselves or others. The group considered the problem of the many differing opinions of the value of allowing children to express anger – which may become uncontrollable. They discussed Jewett's method of helping children to express anger by first modelling the facial expression associated with anger, then acting angrily and finally adding words to the activities. She uses this as a means of aiding the expression of five basic emotions – 'sad, mad, glad, scared and lonely' (Jewett 1984, p 56). The group also considered her use of children's 'energy zones' and her discussion of how children's increased awareness of the natural use of a particular part of their body to express anger can help them in its discharge.

119

I gave the group an outline of ways in which children could be helped to manage the physical release of anger without damage to themselves, to others or to property. These included punching a pillow, tearing newspaper, writing expletives, drawing or painting angry feelings, punching, poking and smashing clay (Owen and Curtis 1983, Oaklander 1978).

One group member told of his experience of these techniques. He had helped a teenage girl to express her anger by spontaneously suggesting that she punch a pillow when she seemed angry. This had brought her relief and relaxation. He told us of his use of 'the angry chair', when he encouraged a child to speak directly to an imaginary person sitting nearby. Finally, he spoke of an experience with a very angry child following a review when the boy had rushed out of the room. The group member had followed him and held him tight, not allowing him to damage himself. He spoke in a way which the group found touching, about how he had held this very distressed boy until his anger gradually died away. The message conveyed to the boy not only verbally but by his actions was of acceptance and concern for his safety. He also helped him manage the emotion, and comforted him with his physical presence.

The group then turned, amid ribald remarks, to attacking clay with great vigour. We punched, poked and squeezed it with increasing ferocity as we might when angry. Furiously we picked it up and slammed it down. Using water to make it smooth and sensuous, the group made it squeak; silky smooth, we stroked it, all amidst very active communication. This proved to be so absorbing that there was no time to review the work of the group and plan for its future. It was as though the group did not want this final session to end. Eventually it did; as a compromise, we agreed to hold a short review session later, to make a formal ending.

Learning Points

From running this group, I added greatly to my knowledge of direct work and communication with children, and gained a conviction of the worth and importance of these methods as an aid to the social worker's role. I enlarged my knowledge of child development, particularly of attachment, sensory development and the ways in which children become 'stuck' at earlier levels of emotional development. With increased understanding of these areas, my effectiveness and confidence as a practitioner has grown.

I have been able to translate the overall knowledge I have gained into practice, working with a ten year old bereaved child, and have been effective in establishing a trusting relationship with him, being aware of his growing attachment to me, understanding the nature of his problems, to which he led me in his play, and helping him to express and understand his feelings.

As a result of my experience, I consider that I now have sufficient resources, both internal and external, to enable me to deal with the pain of children, to understand and work with their experiences and problems, and help them to build up a secure sense of their own self-worth. I learnt too that running a group must not be embarked upon without preparation, planning and organisation. It is also important to remain within the bounds of one's own expertise, and use others skilled in particular areas for consultation and contributions. Finally, any group of this sort must confine its activities and content to topics which fall within the boundaries of social work practice (Goldstein et al 1986).

10 Ending Relationships Successfully

Margaret Adcock, with Dominic Dubois and Andrew Small

When relationships suddenly end and one hasn't a chance to understand why or to say goodbye, it can be an agonizing and harmful experience. Children in care, in particular, are likely to have had many relationships terminated abruptly, and apparently inexplicably. Colón (1981), an American therapist, describing his childhood, wrote:

> When my ten foster brothers left our foster home at different times, there was no opportunity for further contact with them. I experienced their leaving and the permanent cut offs from them as a sense of depression.

In his view, those who experience what he calls unresolved emotional 'cut offs' from significant people in their life are at a higher risk emotionally than those who have resolved such 'cut offs'.

Children in the care system who have not been given an opportunity both to understand the facts and to express their feelings about separation and moving are likely to experience unresolved emotional 'cut offs' of this kind. They may then become 'stuck' (see Chapter 2). Fahlberg (1984) describes them as unable to make use of new experiences and new relationships, often holding themselves responsible for what has happened and consequently feeling worthless, and lacking in self-esteem. Young people who were in care have spoken strongly about their need both to piece together the past and to feel that someone had recognized something positive in them – and had something good to say about them.

Even very young children need explanations about what has happened, and an opportunity to grasp the implications. Yet studies of children in care and leaving care make it clear how often this fails to happen. Stein and Carey, who studied a group of young people leaving care, said that some of the saddest communications from their group were on this subject. One said, 'I know what a parcel feels like in the post. I felt like they had forgotten the address'. They quote Hitchman, who wrote of her experiences in care: 'If reasons and explanations had been given to me, I might have understood. Perhaps they were and I did not understand it but I doubt it. No one thought of giving explanations to small orphans any more than to market bound pigs'. Stein and Carey conclude:

> Two types of knowledge seem to be denied to those in care – one about their movements and the other about their background. Parcels and pigs do not have much sense of identity and, if children are worried about where they come from, they cannot come to terms with themselves and look for a possible future. (Stein and Carey 1986, pp 16–17)

The Social Worker's Task

There are three prerequisites that need attention if social workers are to help children avoid unresolved emotional 'cut offs':
- the unnecessary severing of links must be guarded against;
- factual explanations ought to be given: why does/did the child have to move?
- opportunities ought to occur for the child to express his or her feelings and, wherever possible, share these with the people he or she is leaving or has left.

The crucial times for explanation, communication and discussion are likely to be at admission to care, on changing placement and on leaving care.

The Unnecessary Severing of Links

Many writers have shown how frequently children lose touch with their families when they come into care (Fanshel and Shinn 1978, Aldgate 1980, Millham et al 1986). This might be avoided if social workers recognized the importance of maintaining links, and worked actively to promote this. Parents and relatives closest to the child may feel guilty or distressed by the separation (Jenkins and Norman 1972), and they may find regular visiting very difficult (Aldgate 1976). They may not know what to say or do, or how to respond to those now looking after the child (Millham et al 1986). Unfortunately, what may be a reaction to separation, and feelings of hopelessness or helplessness, may be viewed as a permanent indication of lack of parenting ability. As Atherton (1986a) points out, very little is done to provide the family with

123

practical or psychological support. Emphasis, after the child comes into care, moves away from the family including the child, to the child alone.

It would be of enormous benefit if social workers tried to identify for children coming into care the circle of people who were most important to them, and then explored with those people ways of maintaining links. This circle will often include grandparents and other extended kin, who should not be barred from contact because they have no legal right to it (see Atherton 1986a). *The Code of Practice on Access* (DHSS 1984b) explains very clearly how a social worker can maintain links for children. It stresses the need to encourage regular visiting, which means that birth families and those looking after the children should be told that visiting is beneficial. Social workers need to provide practical assistance with transport and fares, and probably be present themselves on at least the first few occasions to help everyone feel at ease, and smooth out difficulties. Thought needs to be given to the best setting for visits. It may not necessarily be the foster home. It may be necessary to talk beforehand about what the parents will do with their child or children on visits – for example, they can help with meals and bedtimes, playing games etc. In this way everyone can be helped to enjoy at least part of the visit. If it eventually becomes clear that a relationship cannot continue, work needs to be done to help everyone understand why.

Explanation for Moves

Wherever possible, children, whatever their age, need to know beforehand that they will be going away from home or moving to another placement. Repeated explanations and discussions enable information to be absorbed, reducing the risk of misperception and misunderstanding, and helping to diminish the feeling that 'it must be my fault'. This in turn, makes it possible for the child to be more prepared, and feel more in control of the situation. Jewett (1984) suggests that when children feel that moves 'just happen', they may need to reenact the situation in later years in a way that makes them feel in control. This can cause particular problems. For example, a little boy was removed from his parents and their appalling living conditions after a drugs raid. He was subsequently placed in an adoptive family and settled down very well. During his adolescence he suddenly left his adoptive family, and, to their anger and distress, went to live in a squat with drug addicts. He left several months later, apparently more settled, but by then relations with his adoptive family were severely disrupted.

Ideally, children who are moving into care or between placements, or going home after a fairly long absence, should have the opportunity to visit their new home, preferably accompanied by their current carers or parents. Even in a crisis, some preparation can be done. A simple photo album with details of a foster family, for example, can be shared on a car journey to allay fears. Preparation will reduce anxiety, help dispel fantasies and also reinforce reality (Fahlberg 1981b).

Expressing Feelings and Sharing Them with the People Involved

Explanations about moves need to be truthful, but they must also convey to children a recognition and acceptance of the nature of the feelings which they may experience. Some situations may be very distressing, and social workers may need to give a lot of thought to producing statements which reflect this fact but are also helpful to the child. Fahlberg offers a very good example of an explanation given to a four year old about her severe abuse and her separation from her parents.

> Sarah's birth parents started having lots of problems. They were angry with each other much of the time. Sometimes they got angry at Sarah even though, obviously, the problems weren't her fault. One day Mummy Janet got so cross she smacked Sarah much harder than babies should ever be smacked. Afterwards she was sorry. Sarah's leg was badly hurt and she had to stay in hospital for many days. That happened when she was nine months old. At first in the hospital Sarah hurt and she was scared so she cried a lot. When Sarah's mummy and daddy came to see her she would cry like most babies do after they had been away from their mum and dad for a while. However, Mummy Janet and Daddy Tom didn't know that was just how babies act. They thought that the crying meant that Sarah was angry with them. Pretty soon they stopped coming to visit. (Fahlberg 1981b, p 57)

Books about children or animals in similar situations can be very useful in helping to reduce the child's sense of isolation, and his or her feeling that 'it only happens to me'. It may be easier to talk about the feelings of fictitious characters than to talk about oneself. A very useful book is *Joey* (Van der Meer 1980), the story of a little boy who goes to a foster home, which outlines many of the reasons why children come into care and encapsulates their feelings about going from home into an unknown situation. Another is *Bruce's Story* (Thom and Macliver 1986).

125

Wherever possible, children need to talk about going away from the people they are leaving. Very often the adults may be reluctant to do this and may press for children to leave as soon as possible, to minimise their pain and discomfort. Both birth and substitute parents may feel guilty, angry and bereft. If they do not receive help to resolve these feelings, they may subsequently express them in a way which is harmful to the child. Social workers should recognize the importance of this preparation work and press for opportunities to bring it about. If they can achieve it, children are more likely to feel that they have *permission* to move. This will help them settle in their new placement.

Robert, aged 3½, was prepared by his social worker to leave the foster home where he had been for 18 months to go to an adoptive family. The social worker used books, games and dolls to give Robert repeated explanations of why he had to move, and what would happen, allowing him to express his own feelings about it. The new parents became acquainted with him in an intensive series of visits, gradually taking over more and more of Robert's care. The foster mother wanted Robert to have a new 'keeping' family but she was very upset about him going and could not talk to him very much about this.

Just before he was ready to move, the social worker met with Robert, the foster mother and the new adoptive mother. She asked the foster mother to take Robert on her lap and tell him how she felt about his leaving. The foster mother told Robert that she loved him very much and that she was very, very sad he was going. Robert said, 'No, you're not. You're glad because I've been bad'. The adults were all astonished and also very upset. The foster mother talked with Robert about the reasons why he could not stay, and about her own very mixed feelings. Finally, she put Robert on the adoptive mother's lap and said she wanted Robert to learn to love his new mummy even more than he had loved her, and she wanted him to be very happy in his new home. Everyone, including the social worker found this a very painful session, but also a positive one because it helped to make links between the past, the present and the future. After this Robert was quickly able to become strongly attached to his new family.

Working with Pain

If social workers are to help children and adults resolve emotional 'cut offs' and end relationships well, they must feel able to allow anger and pain to be expressed. They must accept that this will be emotionally draining for them personally, but that it is necessary to help the children and the adults with whom they are working. Dominic Dubois describes the effect on him of working with a teenage brother and sister, Jan and Sasha:

Just before I commenced my work Sasha showed her social worker (my co-worker) a suicide note she had written. This led to a long discussion about the despair that Sasha felt. Her wish to write a book about her life then followed. She wanted to chart her life and her continuing feelings of despair. Her social workers responded by wishing to demonstrate that people had cared for her throughout her life. Further, she felt strongly that the department owed Sasha and Jan a huge debt for the poor care provided. I joined with the worker to focus specifically on the work described below.

I completed a chronological history for Sasha and Jan. I found this most painful to do. It gave me the capacity, however, to subsequently share the pain in their lives, another cornerstone of my work. It is no coincidence that I was only able to finish this work after doing a flow chart of my own life. I found that I had the strength to be with Sasha when she learnt about her wish to 'grow up quickly' when aged twelve, so she could return to live with her father, who had told her that she would return home when she grew up. 'I've always been a mug', she commented.

I did, and do, feel frightened at times about telling Sasha and Jan the truth around their mother's desertion. At the same time, I increasingly believe that the truth is better than what they imagine. They can come to terms with reality and thus grow as people, which they cannot do with fantasies, which are, by nature, static.

Dominic Dubois describes how he and his co-worker helped Sasha and Jan to piece together their past, and, through compiling a life story book, express and clarify their mixed feelings about leaving their parents and their carers.

Sasha met the head of the children's home, Miss Ramsay, where they had lived for four years. (This discussion was recorded for Jan.) Sasha learnt three main things from this meeting. Firstly, Miss Ramsay described Sasha as being a tense, anxious, isolated, sensitive child who cried easily, and who did not change over four years. Sasha then shared how she felt herself to be less sensitive now, but still tense and anxious. Secondly, Miss Ramsay made it clear that she was the first person to detect Sasha's deafness and act upon it; Sasha was then nearly four years old. The implications of the lack of stimulation and isolation, as well as neither of her parents noticing her deafness, were not lost on her. Thirdly, Miss Ramsay gave Sasha a balanced account of her father's problems and limitations.

These points were all reinforced when their first social worker, from several years back, met them. In addition, she described Miss Ramsay's strengths and limitations: she provided great stimulation for the children and built up their health, but she did not show affection to them – she cuddled none of them.

Their social worker began to write the life story book with both Sasha and Jan, by writing down the memories of their past. (By this time Jan was also interested in writing a life story book.) Jan recalled essentially factual details, apart from punishments and his conviction that he was never going to live with his father. Sasha recalled emotions, as well as facts: 'I had my hopes I would live with Dad – I must have been crazy. When I was twelvish, it dawned on me that I wasn't going home. I wanted me, Jan and Dad, no one else'.

We explained that we wanted to help them compose the history of their lives, as far as possible, with photogaphs, memories of their own, memories of people who knew them, our own files and from visiting places where they had lived. They were both very interested: Jan brought out photographs of his own; they asked for copies of their birth certificates, and details of their first two placements after reception into care.

They also raised the wish to trace their mother, 'if only to see what she looks like', said Sasha. This wish became increasingly important, to the extent that it became the major focus of our work. It illustrated a significant point: the willingness to let Sasha and Jan lead us to work on what *they* were concerned about.

I was anxious about the effect of trying to trace their mother on Sasha and Jan, but I was reassured by Nessie Bailey's firm conviction that social workers cannot damage children in their direct work any more than they have been already. This same point was repeated by our supervisor in a different form. The reality could not be worse than what they imagined. Even if their mother refused to see them, reasons could be given which would be less damaging than their fantasies.

Responding therefore to Sasha and Jan's wish to learn more about their mother and to try to trace her, my co-worker and I visited their father. Sasha and Jan emphasized that he had always refused to disclose any information. In the event, he was very cooperative and open. We explained our purpose, to help Sasha and Jan to write the story of their lives. We did not focus specifically on their mother but introduced the topic of her during the course of the interview. He clarified the circumstances of her desertion, she had left following a row with *her* father, not with him. Further, and very strikingly, he had never asked what the row was about. Moreover, he talked about his feelings for his first wife: anger and bitterness. Underneath, he seemed very hurt. We did not go to see their father with Sasha and Jan, because they were so sure that he would share so little, and that if he did share anything it would only be without them being there.

Sasha was most interested in what her father had told us about her mother, her mother's desertion and his feelings for her. It came as a surprise to her that we had the strong impression that her father cared for her mother.

I had also been giving Sasha and Jan parts of a chronological summary, starting from the beginning. They would then have a factual history, as well as recorded impressions of them by others. I hoped that these summaries would complement the work which we were doing. For instance, their hopes of being reunited with their father, which they explored with us, could be checked against their words and behaviour during their childhood and adolescence. They now each possess a copy of this summary. I have only removed those parts which would not otherwise respect the confidentiality of their parents.

Sasha continued to be preoccupied about her parents. We therefore arranged for Sasha and Jan to meet with their father and ourselves, so he could share with them what he had shared with us.

In the event, only Sasha came. A fuller picture of her parents' marriage emerged. We now learned they had been under great pressure from their extended family to marry, a pressure which Sasha's father had tried unsuccessfully to resist. Further, he talked about his first wife being 'mental' and 'having no feelings for not having kept in touch with their children'. It should be remembered that this was the first time Sasha had talked with her father about her mother.

Afterwards, Sasha shared her responses. She felt that her father blamed himself, underneath, for what had happened. Her father had done his best in standing by them. She did not think that her mother was 'mental'. She felt that 'half her life' was missing until she had met her mother.

We then visited a maternal aunt. She gave another account of the relationship between Sasha and Jan's parents. Their father had spent almost every evening gambling during their marriage. Their mother was therefore very short of money and neglected the children because she felt so unsupported. She tried to leave but was prevented. Her father then rowed with her because she neglected the children. She then left, not because of the row, but because she could not stand her husband any longer. The aunt had had contact with her eight years ago and offered to try to contact her again. We subsequently shared this with Jan. He knew that his father gambled; it was hard for him, however, to accept his father's weaknesses.

At the time of writing, we have fixed four tasks to do:

1   Their aunt will meet with Sasha and Jan to talk with them about what she told us.
2   This aunt will try to trace their mother.
3   If this fails, a London newspaper is interested in featuring an article, with a photograph, asking for their mother to make contact.
4   We are exploring the possibility of psychotherapy for Sasha.

Our work has helped Sasha and Jan in several ways. They now know many of the reasons why their mother deserted them. This has gone some way towards clarifying their mixed feelings about their parents. They know the facts of their past lives, which satisfies a big need. Sasha is accepting herself, especially her darker side, more, and wishing to explore this further. Jan has gained a lot of confidence: two years ago, he covered his face with his hands rather than speak; now he talks at length and asks questions. They can begin to judge the quality of the care provided by their parents and their carers until the age of eighteen. They are better able to understand why they have never returned to live with their father, why the ending happened in the way it did.

Ending Relationships with Social Workers

It is just as important for social workers to end their relationships well with children as it is to help them finish relationships successfully with other people. It should be a demonstration that people can say goodbye in a non-destructive way, and without a residue of anger or bitter memories. Unfortunately, there are many obstacles to good endings which need to be recognized if the twin pitfalls of abrupt termination or inappropriate continuing contact are to be avoided.

At the beginning of the work, thought needs to be given to the nature and purpose of the relationship between the social worker and the child. Throughout the work, the social worker needs to check with his or her supervisor that this has not been changed. The work needs to be a means to an end, and the relationship finishes when the goals have been achieved.

Defining the Goals

In nearly all cases, the aim of the worker will be to help the child move into a family or to prepare for independent living after care. The worker will need to use the relationship with the child to help the child explore the past, and, simultaneously, experience something different in the present. Mattinson and Sinclair (1979) define this relationship as a limited reliable contact which challenges beliefs about attachment figures. Because the work is likely to arouse very powerful feelings, it is important that the relationship is being used in this way.

Dominic Dubois describes how his supervisor helped him when he and his co-worker did not recognize what was happening in their work. At one point during the preparation of the life story book, because other events had been preoccupying both Sasha and Jan and the workers, construction of the book had lapsed. No plans had been made to restart the work and no date set for further meetings.

> We then failed to set another time to see Sasha. (Jan was in prison.) She came in twice over Christmas, with a request to see a psychiatrist, and saw a previous social worker. She then wrote to my co-worker that she did not wish to continue with her life story work because she did not know when it would end; she did, however, want to trace her mother.
>
> This brought us up short. Our supervisor made several perceptive points, which enlightened my understanding of our work. We had stirred up a lot of feelings; it was easy to underestimate the effect of our work. The delay in seeing them made them feel that their past history was so bad that we did not want to see them again. We should have made our mutual goals more explicit, as well as our time-scale.

Mistakes hurt, but it is possible to really learn from them. We soon saw Sasha again, and subsequently Jan. We apologized. We restated our goals. Sasha shared her concern about whether her father cared for her.

It is equally easy for workers to be too aware of the strength of the relationship and become inappropriately over-involved. Britton (1983) suggests that when family breakdown has occurred, children are psychically 'unplaced'. Children may imagine that a worker has become a parent, or want the worker to be so. The worker may find that this arouses very strong reciprocal feelings. It is absolutely essential that the worker recognizes that he or she cannot become a parent to the child. As Britton points out, the notion that a therapist is providing remedial parenting or a taste of ideal parenthood can lead to intense rivalries, often not consciously perceived as such, between workers and those actually looking after the child.

If worker and child are clear that work is a means to an end, then the final stages will be painful, but not too difficult, as Andrew Small describes in his work with Jason:

> In order for me to help the process of letting go, moving on and transferring attachments, it was important to pay attention to Jason's vulnerability at the ending of this attachment. I did this by paying attention to four main areas of work:
>
> (a)   The first was my need to grieve the loss of Jason, some of which needed to be done with him. I told him that I would miss him, that I was sad that our sessions would not continue but I was glad he was going to his grandmother's to be looked after until he grew up. This enabled Jason to reciprocate how he felt.
>
> (b)   The second was to involve the new carer, i.e. his grandmother, in the plans, by increasing contact with her and ensuring Jason took a full part in this stage of work. Thus Jason knew I had made plans for regular contact with his grandmother, leading up to his final departure. Also Grandmother made a visit (from Birmingham) to see Jason at the Centre in order for him to show her around. This encouraged attachment between them and made the eventual move easier.
>
> (c)   The third was by marking the transition and ending of the work with a celebration at the Centre where the goodbyes were said. Grandmother was an important part of this.

132

(d)   Lastly, to echo for Jason the transitional phenomena, I gave him a soft cap. The cap was intended as a 'transitional object'. This is the name that Winnicott gives to an 'object' used by small children as a halfway reality, between the early state of undifferentiated being and the later stage of true differentiation between subject and object (see Winnicott 1965).

Finally, we used the candle ritual:

You use a row of candles to represent all the people the child has loved in his or her life. In front of this row, you place a candle to symbolize the child. While lighting this candle, you explain that it represents the child's birth, when he or she came into the world with an inborn ability to love people. Next, if it is significant, you light the first candle representing the birth mother and explain that this was the first person the child loved.

You continue the process down the line, lighting a candle for each new situation the child moved into and each new person who was loved. Tell the child that because they were born with the ability to love people it is not necessary to put out (extinguish) the love of the previous carer before loving another.

This technique illustrates how important it is to keep love alive. Usually we only use it when a new family is imminent, for it reveals that it is safe for the child to light the candles belonging to the new family. Once the child is with the new family, we repeat the ritual with the new parents to emphasise how important it is not to extinguish the love the child has for others from the past, because it illuminates the child in the present (Ryan and Walker 1985, p 32).

This ritual demonstrated to Jason that the love and warmth he felt for earlier carers did not have to be 'blown out'! As his attachment was made to his new family a new candle was added and lit alongside the others.

References

ADCOCK, M., 'The Right to a Permanent Placement', *Adoption and Fostering*, vol. 4, no. 1, 1980.

ADCOCK, M., 'Alternatives to Adoption', *Adoption and Fostering*, vol. 8, no. 1, 1984.

ADCOCK, M. and WHITE, R., 'Adoption, Custodianship or Fostering?', *Adoption and Fostering*, vol. 9, no. 4, 1985.

AHMED, S., CHEETHAM, J., and SMALL, J., eds., *Social Work with Black Children and their Families*, Batsford/BAAF, 1986.

AINSWORTH, N.D.S., *Infancy in Uganda*, Johns Hopkins University Press, 1967.

AINSWORTH, N.D.S., 'Attachment: Retrospect and Prospect', in PARKES C.M., and STEVENSON-HINDE, J., eds., *The Place of Attachment in Human Behaviour*, Tavistock, 1982.

ALDGATE, J., 'The Child in Care and his Parents', *Adoption and Fostering*, vol. 84, no. 4, 1976.

ALDGATE, J., 'Identification of Factors Influencing Children's Length of Stay in Care', in TRISELIOTIS, J. ed., *New Developments in Foster Care and Adoption*, Routledge and Kegan Paul, 1980.

ALDGATE, J., 'Making or Breaking Families: the Case for Inclusive Permanence'. Paper given to the Association of Child Psychology and Psychiatry, Cambridge, 1984.

ALDGATE, J. and HAWLEY, D., *Recollections of Disruption*, National Foster Care Association (NFCA), 1986.

ARNOLD, E., 'Finding Black Families for Black Children in Britain', in CHEETHAM, J., ed., *Social Work and Ethnicity*, George Allen and Unwin, 1982.

ATHERTON, C., 'The Importance and Purpose of Access', in *Promoting Links: keeping children and families in touch*, Family Rights Group (FRG), 1986a.

ATHERTON, C., 'The Family's Experience of Difficulties in Access', in ibid, 1986b.

ATHERTON, J.S., *Professional Supervision in Group Care*, Tavistock, 1986.

AUSUBEL, D.P., *Theories and Problems of Adolescent Development*, NY, Grune, Stratton, 1954.

AXLINE, V., *Play Therapy*, Riverside Press, 1947.

REFERENCES

AXLINE, V., *Dibs – In Search of Self*, Riverside Press, 1964.

BALDWIN, J., 'The Black Boy Looks at the White Boy', in Baldwin, J., *The Price of the Ticket*, Michael Joseph, 1985.

BATTY, D., 'The Use of Flow Charts', in British Agencies for Adoption and Fostering, (BAAF), *In Touch with Children*, 1984.

BEEZLEY, P., MARTIN H. and ALEXANDER, H., 'Comprehensive Family Oriented Therapy', in HEFFER, R.E. and KEMPE, C.H., eds., *Child Abuse and Neglect. The Family and the Community*, Ballinger, 1976.

BENIANS, R. 'Preserving Parental Contact: a Factor in Promoting Healthy Growth and Development in Children', in Family Rights Group, ed., *Fostering Parental Contact*, 1982.

BENTOVIM, A., 'Psychiatric Issues', in ADCOCK, M. and WHITE, R., eds., *Terminating Parental Contact*, British Agencies for Adoption and Fostering (BAAF), 1980.

BENTOVIM, A., GORELL BARNES, G., COOKLIN, A., *Family Therapy: Complementary Frameworks of Theory and Practice*, Academic Press, 1982.

BENTOVIM, A., 'A Family Therapy Approach to Making Decisions in Child Care Cases', in BENTOVIM, A. et al, 1982, op. cit.

BION, W., *Learning From Experience*, Heinemann, 1962.

BLACK, D., 'Sundered Families: the Effect of the Loss of a Parent', in *Adoption and Fostering*, vol. 8, no. 2, 1984.

BLOM-COOPER, L., *A Child in Trust*, London Borough of Brent, 1985.

BOSTON, M., and SZUR, R., eds., *Psychotherapy with Severely Deprived Children*, Routledge and Kegan Paul, 1983.

BOSWELL, A., 'Relinquishing', *Adoption and Fostering*, vol. 105, no. 3, 1981.

BOWLBY, J., *Attachment*, (Attachment and Loss vol. 1), Hogarth Press, 1961.

BOWLBY, J., *Separation: Anxiety and Anger*, (Attachment and Loss vol. 2), Hogarth Press, 1973.

BOWLBY, J., *Loss: Sadness and Depression*, (Attachment and Loss vol. 3), Hogarth Press, 1980.

BOWLBY, J., 'The Making and Breaking of Affectional Bonds', in BAAF, ed., *Working with Children*, 1986.

BOWLBY, J., *The Making and Breaking of Affectional Bonds*, Social Science Paperbacks, Tavistock, 1979.

BRETHERTON, I. and WATERS, E., eds., *Growing Points of Attachment Theory and Research*, Monograph of the Society for Research in Child Development, vol. 50, nos. 1–2, 1985.

BRITISH AGENCIES FOR ADOPTION AND FOSTERING (BAAF), ed., *In Touch with Children – A Training Pack*, 1984.

BRITISH AGENCIES FOR ADOPTION AND FOSTERING (*BAAF*), ed., *Working with Children*, 1986.

BRITISH ASSOCIATION OF SOCIAL WORKERS, *Guidelines for Practice in Family Practice*, 1982.

BRITTON, R. 'Breakdown and Reconstitution of the Family Circle' in BOSTON, M. and SZUR, R., eds., op. cit.

BROWN, C., *Black and White Britain: the Third PSI Survey*, Heinemann, 1984.

CHEETHAM, J., *Social Work with Immigrants*, Routledge and Kegan Paul, 1972.

CHEETHAM, J., ed., *Social Work and Ethnicity*, George Allen and Unwin, 1982.

136

CHEETHAM, J., 'Introduction', in AHMED, S. et al, 1986 op cit.

CLARK, K.B. and M.P., 'Racial Identification and Preferences in Negro Children', in NEWCOME, T., HARTLEY, E., eds., *Readings in Social Psychology*, Heimholt, 1974.

CLARKE, A.M. and CLARKE, A.D.B., *Early Experience: Myth and Evidence*, Open Books, 1976.

COLLINS, T., and BRUCE, T., *Staff Support and Staff Training*, Tavistock, 1986.

COLON, F., 'In Search of One's Past: an identity trip', *Family Process*, vol. 12, 1973.

COLON, F., 'Family Ties and Child Placement' in SINANOGLU, P. and MALUCCIO, A., eds., *Parents of Children in Placement – Perspectives and Programmes*, Child Welfare League of America, 1981.

COOPER, S., 'A Look at the Effect of Racism on Clinical Work', *Social Casework*, February 1973.

COOPER, C., 'The Growing Child', in BAAF, ed., 1986, op. cit.

CURTIS, P., 'Communicating Through Play'. Paper given to BAAF seminar, Working with Children, London, October 1981, extracted in *Adoption and Fostering*, vol. 6, no. 1, 1982.

DAVEY, A.G. et al, 'Who Would You Most Like to Be?', *New Society*, September 25, 1980.

DEARNLEY, B., 'A Plain Man's Guide to Supervision – or New Clothes for the Emperor?', *Journal of Social Work Practice*, November 1985.

DHSS, *Foster Care: A Guide to Practice*, HMSO, 1976.

DHSS, *Report of the House of Commons Social Services Committee*, HMSO, 1984a.

DHSS, *Code of Practice on Access to Children in Care*, HMSO, 1984b.

DHSS, *Social Work Decisions in Child Care*, HMSO, 1986.

DINNAGE, R. and KELLMER PRINGLE, M., *Residential Child Care: Facts and Fallacies*, Longmans, 1967.

DOCKAR-DRYSDALE, B.E., 'The process of symbolization observed among emotionally deprived children in therapeutic school', in TOD, R.J.N., ed., *Disturbed Children*, Longmans, 1968.

DONLEY, K., 'The Dynamics of Disruption', *Adoption and Fostering*, vol. 92, no. 2, 1978.

DORFMAN, E., 'Play Therapy', in ROGERS, C.R., *Client Centred Therapy*, Houghton Mifflin, 1965.

DOUGLAS, T., *Groupwork Practice*, Tavistock, 1976.

DUMMETT, A., *Portrait of Racism in the United Kingdom*, Penguin, 1973.

ERICKSON, E.H., *Identity: Youth and Crisis*, Norton, 1968.

ERICKSON, E.H., 'The Problem of Ego Identity', in *Psychological Issues I*, New York International Universities Press, 1969.

ESSEX SOCIAL SERVICES DEPARTMENT, *Foster Home Breakdown Survey*, 1982.

FAHLBERG, V., *Attachment and Separation*, British Agencies for Adoption and Fostering (BAAF), 1981a.

FAHLBERG, V., *Helping Children When They Must Move*, British Agencies for Adoption and Fostering (BAAF), 1981b.

FAHLBERG, V., *Child Development*, British Agencies for Adoption and Fostering (BAAF), 1982.

FAHLBERG, V., 'The Child who is Stuck', in ADCOCK, M. and WHITE, R. eds., *In*

Touch with Parents, British Agencies for Adoption and Fostering (BAAF), 1984.

FANSHEL, D. and SHINN, E.B., *Children in Foster Care: a Longitudinal Investigation*, Columbia University Press, 1978.

FAMILY RIGHTS GROUP, *Fostering Parental Contact*, 1982.

FISHER, M., MARSH, P., PHILLIPS, D., SAINSBURY, E.E., *In and Out of Care – The Experiences of Children, Parents and Social Workers*, Batsford/BAAF, 1986.

FITZGERALD, J., *Understanding Disruption*, British Agencies for Adoption and Fostering (BAAF), 1983.

FITZGERALD, J., MURCER, B. and MURCER, B., *Building New Families*, Blackwell, 1982a.

FITZGERALD, J., MURCER, B., and MURCER, B., 'Building New Families', *Adoption and Fostering*, vol. 6, no. 3, 1982b.

FITZHERBERT, K., *West Indian Children in London*, Bell, 1967.

FORSTER, J., *Divorce Conciliation*, Scottish Council for Single Parents, 1982.

FOSTER-CARTER, O., 'Insiders, Outsiders and Anomalies; A Review of Studies of Identity', *New Community*, vol. 13, no. 2, 1986.

FOX, L., 'Two Value Positions in Recent Child Care Law and Practice', *British Journal of Social Work*, vol. 12, 1982.

FRATTER, J., NEWTON, D., SHINEGOLD, D., *Cambridge Cottage Pre-Fostering and Adoption Unit*, Barnardo's Papers, no. 16, 1982.

GAMBRILL, E.D. and STEIN, T.J., 'Decision Making and Case Management: Achieving Continuity of Care for Children in Out of Home Placement' in MALUCCIO, A.N. and SINANOGLU, P.A., *Partnership with Parents: Working with Parents of Children in Foster Care*, Child Welfare League of America, 1981.

GAMBRILL, E.D., *Casework: A Competency-Based Approach*, Prentice Hall, 1983.

GEORGE, V., *Foster Care Theory and Practice*, Routledge and Kegan Paul, 1970.

GILL, O. and JACKSON, B., *Adoption and Race*, Batsford/BAAF, 1983.

GOLDSTEIN, J., FREUD, A., SOLNIT, A., *Beyond the Best Interests of the Child*, Free Press, 1973.

GOLDSTEIN, J., FREUD, A., SOLNIT, A., GOLDSTEIN, S., *In the Best Interests of the Child*, Free Press, 1986.

HAIMES, E. and TIMMS, N., *Adoption, Identity and Social Policy: the Search for Distant Relatives*, Gower, 1985.

HAPGOOD, M., 'Older Child Adoption and the Knowledge Base of Adoption Practice', in BEAN, P., ed., *Adoption: Essays in Social Policy, Law and Sociology*, Tavistock Publishing, 1984.

HARINGEY SOCIAL SERVICES DEPARTMENT, *Study of Attitudes of Long Term Foster Parents who have Ceased Fostering*, 1982.

HARRIS, J., 'An Introduction to Attachment Theory and its Place in Child Care Practice', in BAAF 1986, op. cit.

HAWORTH, M.R., and KELLER, M.J., 'The Use of Food in Therapy', in HAWORTH, M.R., ed., *Child Psychotherapy – Practice and Teaching*, Basic Books, 1964.

HEINIKE, C.M. and WESTHEIMER, I.J., *Brief Separations*, Longmans, 1965.

HENRY, G. 'Doubly Deprived', in DAWS, D. and BOSTON, M., eds., *The Child Psychotherapist*, Wildwood House, 1981.

HENSEY, O.J., WILLIAMS, J.K. and ROSENBLOOM, L., 'Intervention in Child Abuse: Experience in Liverpool', in *Developmental Medicine and Child Neurology*, 1983.

HERBERT, M., *Caring for your Children*, Blackwell, 1985.

HERBERT, M. and SLUCKIN, W. and SLUCKIN, A., 'Mother-to-Infant Bonding' in *Journal of Child Psychology and Psychiatry*, vol. 23, no. 2, 1982.

HETHERINGTON, E.M., 'Children and Divorce', in HENDERSON, R., ed., *Parent-Child Interaction*, Academic Press, 1980.

HITCHMAN, J., *King of the Barbareens*, Patman, 1966.

HOLMAN, R., 'The Place of Fostering in Social Work', *British Journal of Social Work*, vol. 5, no. 1, 1975.

HORNE, J., 'When the Social Worker is a Bridge', in Sawbridge, P., ed., *Parents for Children*, British Agencies for Adoption and Fostering (BAAF), 1983.

HUDSON, B.L. and MACDONALD, G.M., *Behavioural Social Work – An Introduction*, Macmillan, 1986.

HUSBAND, C., 'Racism, Prejudice and Social Policy', in COMBE, V., and LITTLE, A., *Race and Social Work: A Guide to Training*, Tavistock Publications, 1986.

JACKSON, A.D. and DUNNE, M.J., 'Permanency Planning in Foster Care with the Ambivalent Parent', in MALUCCIO, A.N. and SINANOGLU, P.A., op. cit, 1981.

JENKINS, S., 'The Tie that Bonds', in ibid.

JENKINS, S., 'The American Ethnic Dilemma', in CHEETHAM, J., ed., 1982, op. cit.

JENKINS, S., and NORMAN, E., *Filial Deprivation and Foster Care*, Columbia University Press, 1972.

JEWETT, C., *Helping Children Cope with Separation and Loss*, Batsford/BAAF, 1984.

JEWETT, C., 'Adoption and Adolescence', unpublished paper given at a seminar organised by Parents for Children, September 1986.

KADUSHIN, A., *Adopting Older Children*, Columbia University Press, 1970.

KAFFMAN, M. and ELIZIR, E., 'Bereavement Responses of Kibbutz and non-Kibbutz Children Following the Death of the Father', *Journal of Child Psychology and Psychiatry*, vol. 23, no. 3, 1983.

KEANE, A., 'Behaviour Problems among Long-Term Foster Children', Adoption and Fostering, vol. 7, no. 3, 1983.

KELLMER PRINGLE, M., *The Needs of Children*, Hutchinson, 1975.

KELLY, G., 'Research: family contact in Northern Ireland', *Adoption and Fostering*, vol. 9, no. 4, 1985.

KENT, B., 'The Social Worker's Cultural Pattern as it Affects Casework with Immigrants', in TRISELIOTIS, J., 1972, op cit.

KLINE, D. and OVERSTREET, H.M.F., *Foster Care of Children: Nurture and Treatment*, Columbia University Press, 1972.

KUBLER-ROSS, E., *Death and Dying*, Tavistock Publications, 1972.

LAMBERT, L., 'Adopted from Care by the Age of Seven', *Adoption and Fostering*, vol. 5, no. 3, 1981.

LEIGH, J.W. and GREEN, J.W., 'The Structure of the Black Community: the Knowledge Base for Social Services', in GREEN, W., ed., *Cultural Awareness in the Human Services*, Prentice-Hall, 1982.

LIGHTBOWN, C., 'Life Story Books', *Adoption and Fostering*, vol. 97, no. 3, 1979.

LIM, S.P., 'Loss – From the Chinese Point of View', in British Association of Social Workers (BASW), *Loss, Proceedings of the British Association of Social Workers' Summer School on Loss*, 1983.

LITTLE, A., interviewed in *Roots*, October/November, vol. 6, no. 5, 1979.

LOGAN, S.L., 'Race, Identity and Black Children: A Developmental Perspective', *Social Casework*, January 1981.

LYNCH, M., 'Ill Health and Child Abuse' in *The Lancet*, no. 2, 1975.

LYNCH, M., and ROBERTS, J., *Consequences of Child Abuse*, Academic Press, 1982.

MADGE, N., 'Identifying Families at Risk', in MADGE, N. ed., *Families at Risk*, Heinemann, 1983.

MANN, P., *Children in Care Revisited*, Batsford/BAAF, 1984.

MARTIN, H., ed., 'Factors influencing the Abused Child', in *The Abused Child*, Ballinger, 1976.

MARTIN, H. and BEEZLEY, P., 'Behavioural Observation of Abused Children', *Developmental Medicine and Child Neurology*, no. 19, 1977.

MACLEOD, V., *Whose Child?*, Occasional Papers, No. 11, Study Commission on the Family, 1983.

MALUCCIO, A.N., FEIN, E. and HAMILTON, J., KLIER, J.L., and WARD, D., 'Beyond Permanency Planning', *Child Welfare*, vol. 49, no. 3, 1980.

MALUCCIO, A.N. and SINANOGLU, P.A., *Partnership with Parents: working with parents of children in foster care*, Columbia University Press, 1981.

MALUCCIO, A.N., FEIN, E. and OLMSTEAD, K.A., *Permanency Planning for Children*, Tavistock Publications, 1986.

MARRIS, P., *Loss and Change*, Routledge and Kegan Paul, 1974.

MATTINSON, J., *The Reflection Process in Casework Supervision*, Institute of Marital Studies, 1975.

MATTINSON, J ., and SINCLAIR, I., *Mate and Stalemate*, Blackwell, 1979.

MAXIME, J.E., 'Some Psychological Models of Black Self-Concept', in AHMED et al, 1986, op. cit.

MILLHAM, S., BULLOCK, R., HOSIE, K. and HAAK, M., *Lost in Care*, Gower, 1985.

MILNER, D., *Children and Race*, Penguin, 1975.

MITCHELL, J., 'Letters from a Kangaroo: A Third Object Technique for Working with the Young Child', *British Journal of Social Work*, vol. 11, 1981.

MOSTYN, D. 'In Search of Ethnic Identity', *Social Casework*, May 1972.

NAPIER, H., 'Success and Failure in Foster Care', *British Journal of Social Work*, vol. 2, no. 2, 1972.

NORFOLK SOCIAL SERVICES DEPARTMENT, *Report on the Survey of Foster Care in the County*, Report number 183.

OAKLANDER, V., *Windows to our Children*, Real People Press, 1978.

ORBACH, I., GROSS, Y., GLAUBMAN, H. and BERMAN, D., 'Children's

Perceptions of Death in Humans and Animals as a Function of Age Anxiety and Cognitive Ability', *Journal of Child Psychology and Psychiatry*, vol. 26, no. 3, 1985.

ORMROD, R., 'Child Care Law: a Personal Perspective', *Adoption and Fostering*, vol. 7, no. 4, 1983.

OWEN, P. and CURTIS, P., *Techniques for Working with Children*, Owen and Curtis, 1983.

PACKMAN, J., RANDALL, J., JACQUES, N., *Who Needs Care?*, Blackwell, 1986.

PAGE, R. and CLARKE, G.A., eds., *Who Cares?*, National Children's Bureau, 1977.

PARKER, R.A., *Decision in Child Care*, George Allen and Unwin, 1966.

PARKER, R.A., 'Planning into Practice', in *Adoption and Fostering*, vol. 9, no. 4, 1985.

PARSLOE, P., *Social Services Area Teams*, George Allen and Unwin, 1981.

PERLS, F., HEFFERLINE, R.F., GOODMAN, P., *Gestalt Therapy*, Delta, 1951.

QUINTON, D. and RUTTER, M., 'Parents with Children in Care – II, Intergenerational Continuities', *Journal of Child Psychology and Child Psychiatry*, vol. 25, 1984.

RAPOPORT, R., FOGARTY, M. and RAPOPORT, R.N., eds., *Families in Britian*, Routledge and Kegan Paul, 1982.

Report of a Committee of Inquiry into the Care and Supervision Provided in Relation to Maria Colwell, HMSO, 1974.

RICHARDS, M.P.M. and DYSON, M., *Separation, Divorce and the Development of Children: a Review*, Department of Health and Social Security, HMSO, 1982.

RICKS, M., 'The Social Transmission of Parental Behaviour; Attachment across Generations', in BRETHERTON, I. and WATERS, E., eds., *Growing Points of Attachment Theory and Research*, Monographs of the Society for Research in Child Development, vol. 50, nos. 1–2, 1985.

ROWE, J. and LAMBERT, L., *Children Who Wait*, Association of British Adoption and Fostering Agencies (ABAFA), 1973.

ROWE, J., CAIN, H., HUNDLEBY, M. and KEANE, A., *Long-Term Fostering*, Batsford/BAAF, 1984.

RUSHTON, A. and TRESEDER, J., 'Research: Developmental Recovery', *Adoption and Fostering*, vol. 10, no. 3, 1986.

RUTTER, M., *Maternal Deprivation Reassessed*, Penguin, 1972.

RUTTER, M., 'Stress, Coping and Development: Some Issues and Some Questions', *Journal of Child Psychology and Psychiatry*, vol. 22, no. 4, 1981.

RUTTER, M., 'Resilience in the Face of Adversity', *British Journal of Psychiatry*, vol. 147, 1985.

RUTTER, M. and QUINTON, D., 'Long-Term Follow-up of Women Institutional-ized in Childhood: Factors Promoting Good Functioning in Adult Life', *British Journal of Developmental Psychology*, vol. 18, 1984.

RYAN, T. and WALKER, R., *Making Life Story Books*, British Agencies for Adoption and Fostering (BAAF), 1985.

SAWBRIDGE, P., *Parents for Children*, BAAF, 1983.

SCHAFFER, H.R., *Mothering*, Open Books, 1977.

SCHAFFER, H.R. and EMERSON, P.E., *The Development of Social Attachments in*

141

Infancy, Monographs of Social Research in Child Development, vol. 29, no. 4, 1964.

SCHNEIDER ROSEN K., BRAUNWALD, K., CARLSON, V. and CICCHETTI, D., 'Current Perspective in Attachment Theory: Illustration from the Study of Maltreated Infants' in BRETHERTON, I., and WATERS, E., eds., 1985, op. cit, *Attachment Theory and Research*, Monographs of the Society for Research in Child Development, vol. 50, nos. 1–2, 1985.

SELIGMAN, M.E.P., *Helplessness: on Depression, Development and Death*, W.H. Freeman, 1975.

SHAW, M. and LEBENS, K., *What Shall We Do with the Children?* Association of British Adoption and Fostering Agencies (ABAFA), 1978.

SHERIDAN, M., 'Chart Illustrating the Developmental Progress of Infants and Young Children', in British Agencies for Adoption and Fostering (BAAF), 1986, op. cit.

SHINEGOLD, D., review of LENNOX, D., *Residential Group Therapy for Children*, Tavistock Publications, *Adoption and Fostering*, vol. 7, no. 1, 1983.

SKUSE, D., 'Extreme Deprivation in Early Childhood – II. Theoretical Issues and a Comparative Review', *Journal of Child Psychology and Psychiatry*, vol. 25, no. 4, 1984.

SMALL, J., 'Transracial Placements: Conflicts and Contradictions', in AHMED, S. et al, op. cit.

SMALL, J., 'The Crisis in Adoption', in Burke, A., ed., *Transcultural Psychiatry: Racism and Mental Illness*, Avenue Publishing, 1984.

SMITH, D., *Racial Disadvantage in Britain*, Penguin, 1977.

SMITH, D., *The Facts of Racial Disadvantage*, P.E.P., 1976.

SOOTHILL, K. and DERBYSHIRE, M., 'Retaining Foster Parents', *Adoption and Fostering*, vol. 5, no. 2, 1981.

STACEY, M., DEARDEN, R., PIL, R. and ROBINSON, D. *Hospitals, Children, and their Families: the Report of a Pilot Study*, Routledge and Kegan Paul, 1970.

STEIN, M. and CAREY, K., *Leaving Care*, Blackwell, 1986.

STEIN, M. and ELLIS, S., *Gizza Say?*, National Association of Young People in Care (NAYPIC), 1983.

STEVENSON, O., 'Reception into Care – Its Meaning for all Concerned', in TOD, R.J.N., *Children in Care*, Longmans, 1968.

SYLVA, K. and LUNT, I., *Child Development – a First Course*, Grant McIntyre, 1982.

TAJFEL, H., 'Social Identity and Intergroup Behaviour', *Social Science Information*, vol. 13, no. 2, 1974.

TAJFEL, H., 'The Social Psychology of Minorities', in HUSBAND, C., ed., *Race in Britain, Continuity and Change*, Hutchinson University Press, 1982.

THOBURN, J., 'What Kind of Permanence?', *Adoption and Fostering*, vol. 9, no. 4, 1985.

THOBURN, J., MURDOCK, A., and O'BRIEN, A., 'Routes to Permanence', *Adoption and Fostering*, vol. 9, no. 1, 1985.

THOBURN, J., MURDOCK, A. and O'BRIEN, A., *Permanence in Child Care*, Blackwell, 1986.

THORPE, R., *The Social and Psychological Situation of the Long-Term Foster Child with Regard to His Natural Parents*. Unpublished Ph.D. Thesis, University of Nottingham, 1974.

THORPE, R., 'The Experience of Children and Parents Living Apart', in TRISELIOTIS, J., ed., *New Developments in Foster Care and Adoption*, Routledge and Kegan Paul, 1980.

TIBBENHAM, A., 'Fostering in South Devon, A Study of Terminations of Placement', *Clearing House Journal*, University of Birmingham, 1982.

TIZARD, B., *Adoption: A Second Chance*, Open Books, 1977.

TIZARD, B. and HODGES, J., 'The Effect of Early Institutional Rearing on the Development of Eight Year Old Children', *Journal of Child Psychology and Psychiatry*, vol. 19, 1978.

THOM, M. and MACLIVER, C., *Bruce's Story*, The Children's Society, 1986.

TRASLER, G., *In Place of Parents*, Routledge and Kegan Paul, 1960.

TRISELIOTIS, J., *Social Work with Coloured Immigrants and their Families*, Oxford University Press, 1972.

TRISELIOTIS, J., *In Search of Origins*, Routledge and Kegan Paul, 1980.

TRISELIOTIS, J., ed., *New Developments in Foster Care and Adoption*, Routledge and Kegan Paul, 1980.

TRISELIOTIS, J. and RUSSELL, J., *Hard to Place: the Outcome of Adoption and Residential Care*, Heinemann Educational, 1984.

TRISELIOTIS, J., 'Identity and Security', *Adoption and Fostering*, vol. 7, no. 1, 1983.

TRISELIOTIS, J., 'Adoption with Contact', in *Adoption and Fostering*, vol. 9, no. 4, 1985.

VAN DER MEER, R. and A., *Joey*. Heinemann and National Foster Care Association (NFCA), 1980.

WALLERSTEIN, J.S. and KELLY, J.B., *Surviving the Break-Up: How Children and Parents Cope with Divorce*, Grant McIntyre, 1980.

WEDGE, P. and THOBURN, J., eds., *Finding Families for 'Hard to Place' Children – Evidence from Research*, British Agencies for Adoption and Fostering (BAAF), 1986.

WEINSTEIN, E., *The Self-Image of the Child*, Russell Sage Foundation, 1960.

WEST, D., 'Fostering and Adoption Disruptions in Strathclyde', *Adoption and Fostering*, vol. 6, no. 4, 1982.

WEST, J., 'Play Therapy with Rosy', *British Journal of Social Work*, vol. 13, 1983.

WHITTAKER, J.K. 'Family Involvement in Residential Treatment', in MALUCCIO, A.N. and SINANOGLU, P.A., 1981, op. cit.

WINNICOTT, C., 'Communicating with Children', extracted in *Social Work Today*, vol. 8, no. 2, 1977.

WINNICOTT, C., 'Face to Face with Children', in BAAF, ed., 1986, op. cit.

WINNICOTT, D.W., *The Maturational Process and the Facilitating Environment*, Hogarth, 1965.

WOLKIND, S.N., 'A Child Psychiatrist in Court: Using the Contributions of Developmental Psychology', in BRITISH AGENCIES FOR ADOPTION AND FOSTERING, (BAAF), ed., *Taking a Stand*, 1984.

WOLKIND, S.N. and RUTTER, M., 'Children Who Have Been in Care – an Epidemiological Study', *Journal of Child Psychology and Psychiatry*, vol. 14, 1973.

REFERENCES

ZEITLIN, H., review of BENTOVIM, A., GORRELL BARNES, G., COOKLIN, A., *Family Therapy: Complementary Frameworks of Theory and Practice*, Academic Press, 1982, *Adoption and Fostering*, vol. 7, no. 1, 1983.

Index